Advance Praise

"Miriam Plotinsky skillfully weaves together theory and practice in *Writing Their Future Selves*. Through stories and research, Plotinsky makes a compelling case for teachers to focus on academic identity, and the book is bursting with strategies and templates so you can get started immediately. Anyone who writes with students (which is all of us teachers!) should pick up this book to enliven their classrooms and spark their students' creativity and skills."

—**Alex Shevrin Venet,** author of *Equity-Centered Trauma-Informed Education*

"What I love most about *Writing Their Future Selves* is how Miriam Plotinsky weaves relationships and care into all the strategies she shares. These strategies teach students how to express themselves in authentic and meaningful ways. A must-read!"

—**Jon Bergmann,** teacher, author, and Flipped Learning pioneer

"*Writing Their Future Selves* is a treasure trove of insight. Grounded in Plotinsky's years of experience as a teacher and instructional specialist, this book achieves an engaging balance of anecdotes, research, and use-tomorrow strategies that make it valuable to any teacher who works with writers. New teachers will enjoy the mentorship of a master educator and veteran teachers will feel reenergized to transcend myths and stereotypes, and skillfully assist each writer before them."

—**Brett Vogelsinger,** English teacher and author of *Poetry Pauses: Teaching With Poems to Elevate Student Writing in All Genres*

"Years of remote and hybrid instruction due to the COVID-19 pandemic left their mark of separation upon our students. However, in typical fashion, Miriam Plotinsky has authored *Writing Their Future Selves: Instructional Strategies to Affirm Student Identity* to build a bridge that our students can navigate with us teachers, and to strengthen our collective sense of self."

—**Joseph S. Pizzo,** middle school English teacher and adjunct professor, writing department, Centenary University

"In the uncertainty of the post-pandemic era, we as educators have had to rediscover and reinvent ourselves; thus, it should not be surprising that we must also help students identify and cultivate the traits they desire within themselves. *Writing Their Future Selves* shares how teacher temperament and approach can disrupt deficit thinking, affirm identity, and encourage something that students and staff alike must always seek to do: develop self-efficacy."

—**Daryl C. Howard, PhD,** equity instructional specialist

"Whether you are a novice or veteran teacher, *Writing Their Future Selves* offers insights, tools, stories, and questions to bolster student academic identity and confidence. Dive into writing activities that are at home in English Language Arts classes and beyond to connect students with each other, adults, school, and academic content. I appreciate Miriam Plotinsky's conversational style as she supports and guides readers through reflection and instructional moves."

—**Nicholas A. Emmanuele,** English teacher,
Millcreek Township School District

WRITING THEIR FUTURE SELVES

WRITING THEIR FUTURE SELVES

Instructional Strategies to Affirm Student Identity

Miriam Plotinsky

Norton Professional Books

An Imprint of W. W. Norton & Company
Celebrating a Century of Independent Publishing

Note to Readers: Models and/or techniques described in this volume are illustrative or are included for general informational purposes only; neither the publisher nor the author(s) can guarantee the efficacy or appropriateness of any particular recommendation in every circumstance. As of press time, the URLs displayed in this book link or refer to existing sites. The publisher and author are not responsible for any content that appears on third-party websites.

For information about permission to reproduce selections from this book, write to Permissions, W. W. Norton & Company, Inc., 500 Fifth Avenue, New York, NY 10110

For information about special discounts for bulk purchases, please contact W. W. Norton Special Sales at specialsales@wwnorton.com or 800-233-4830

Manufacturing by Kingery Printing Company
Production manager: Gwen Cullen

ISBN: 978-1-324-05285-2 (pbk)

W. W. Norton & Company, Inc., 500 Fifth Avenue, New York, N.Y. 10110
www.wwnorton.com

W. W. Norton & Company Ltd., 15 Carlisle Street, London W1D 3BS

1 2 3 4 5 6 7 8 9 0

*To all the students who taught me that
if you write, you are a writer.*

And to Kenny—with all my love.

Contents

Foreword

We are only afforded a small plot of land in this life, but as Candide reminds us, "the little piece of ground yielded a plentiful crop." Gardens are sometimes beautiful, dressing in the vibrant colors of spring. Other times, gardens are dead, suffering the harsh realities of winter. And often, gardens are somewhere in between—always moving, changing, growing— like those that tend them.

Gardens require constant attention and careful work. The art of gardening takes patience and consistency. A patch of land must constantly be revisited, reworked, and revised to produce the intended result. Adjustments need to be made. Things must be added or taken away in proper proportion. The purpose of a garden varies—some are for nourishment, others are for beauty, some are for enjoyment, and others still are for a quiet place of repose. And in the end, every garden will be different, will be what that gardener makes of it, and will be artistic and elegant in its own way.

Writers are, at best, gardeners. Their tools are simple. A clear head and steady hands do most of the work. No sitting and philosophizing life's great quandaries is required. There is only rolling up sleeves and getting hands dirty. There is much to toil. Only under the right conditions will the results yield what is designed, planned, and executed. Hopefully, we each get what we needed, at least.

So what is a fertile patch of land if not a bidding? What is rich soil sifting through one's fingers if not an overture? What is a blank piece of paper if not an invitation? What is a lonely cursor blinking on a doc if not a calling-in?

As educational institutions, our understanding and implementation of writing instruction, across all disciplines, has lacked focus, care, and vision. The fallout is that individual teachers—who have also been shaped by that paucity of institutional understanding—are led to deficit mindsets about themselves as writing instructors. Such deficit thinking seeps into the writing instruction itself, and ultimately into the writers sitting in our classrooms. This process has been cyclical for generations. Institutional deficit thinking creates individual deficit thinking. For too many years, too many teachers have been stripped of the necessary tools to cultivate writers and the love of writing. Without the necessary tools, the planted seeds do not grow to their intention. Instead, they grow into writing instructors who do not know how to nurture writers. They continue to toil, continue to work hard; they are exhausted, drained by their efforts, but still their crop lacks the fruit they hoped would emerge. What we've seen for many years are writing instructors who know how to assign writing, but few who were ever taught how to teach writing. These structures are overwhelmingly oppressive to our students, our apprentice gardeners. They, too, toil, doing the best with the tools they are given. But liberation is possible. We have hope in our collective future. Because we are the ones who created these oppressive structures and conditions, we can be the ones to dismantle them. Our classrooms and the pedagogies we adopt, much like gardens, offer the eternal possibility of rejuvenation and renewal.

Too often we think (and express to students) that writing is a method of demonstrating what one knows. The result is that students, instead of writing, merely try to get the correct answer—or at least the one they think the teacher wants to read. More frequently, we should offer students writing without focusing on their being right. We need to help students see the ways that writing can be used to figure out what one thinks, not just to demonstrate final thinking. Writing should be a vehicle that helps kids understand their own thinking patterns. Writing should be an opportunity for students to think about big ideas and respond to them. Writing should be about self-expression regarding a definitive purpose to a specific audience. Too often in writing instruction, these are all narrowly manufactured, resulting in equally narrow pieces of writing which can only be measured on a rubric whose criteria is assignment specific, and not intrinsically related to the overall cultivation of the writer.

We sacrifice authenticity for the convenience of teaching grammar and mechanics, which is far easier than refining voice, helping students select an audience beyond their instructor, or developing coherence throughout a piece of writing. Because who cares if all the commas are in the right place if you have nothing to say? Since so many writing instructors were never taught how to teach writing, they teach the same way they were taught. Writing instructors are not copyeditors, but somewhere along the way, we lost sight of that. If we are only bombarding students with the mistakes they make—mostly in grammar and mechanics—then we are developing in students the feeling that writing is something they do wrong, which leads kids to not want to write, which leads to kids who don't write. We can find a better way.

Every student deserves to hone their writing abilities, because such a course of development helps shape their own cognition, which will serve them well as human beings far beyond the classroom. But the ability to hone one's abilities is trapped within the confines of poor writing instruction. Let's name rigid structures and inflexible rules for what they are: white Western culture's way of allowing only a few to be seen as good writers, which in turn dehumanizes and destroys the joy, development, and dreams of so many others. Imagine laboring intensely and crafting a sentence in a language that is not your mother tongue, which opens like a flower bud, revealing a beautiful idea, only to be told that two words are misspelled and the whole thing is a comma splice. Our writing classrooms should provide the freedom to uplift historically marginalized voices. As writing instructors, we should champion the dismissed and the silenced. And we must always remember that quiet doesn't mean "has nothing to say." Too often we inaccurately conflate the two; more often, quiet merely means "chronically ignored by teachers," is a learned state of avoidance because of stereotype threat, or is a survival skill in a world of hazards against perceived linguistic ineptitudes. A withering, or even death, of the writing soul. But we can water that writing soul, nourish it, and help it find its place in the sun.

Writing holds within itself an opportunity to heal, collectively and individually. To approach this lofty ideal, we must cultivate classrooms built on relational trust. A writing classroom must be a community garden, a place where everyone is welcome and where everyone feels like they belong. Part of the beauty of a community garden is that people can plant what they like, and others can take what they need. How do our writing collaboratives reflect this? Are we giving every plant the same amount of water, even though each has individual needs? If all plants get the same amount of nitrogen, phosphorus, potassium, calcium, and magnesium, some will flourish, some will struggle, and some will die. We must determine what the writers in our spaces need and then work to provide them exactly that. One thing that all plants—and all young writers—need, though, is care. And care comes in many forms. In writing, care might look like allowing students to choose the mode of writing that bests aligns with their need for expression on a given topic, or the way instructors establish a feedback loop that concurrently challenges and affirms our writers. Our uplift should be consistent. Our messaging should let kids know, without any doubt, that we want to hear their ideas—that they matter and deserve to be heard. We want students to know that we care about their ideas regardless of the deftness with which they are expressed. We must focus on positive feedback, both teacher-to-student and peer-to-peer, to help young writers increase their confidence, and find joy in writing.

Much of what I'm talking about here is too ethereal, too impermanent, too metaphorical. But there is a solution in your hands. The brilliant work Miriam Plotinsky has done in *Writing Their Future Selves* will move everything towards the tangible, concrete, and actionable in your classroom. Contained in these pages are fundamental, verifiable strategies that will empower your students and move them ever closer to their future writing selves. You will find strategies that you can use in your classroom tomorrow, and they are strategies that can transform your relationship with writing itself, with yourself as a writing instructor, and with your students as writers. As you read this book, consider how such teacher-moves uplift and promote our young writers as fully formed human beings, though they are still young and ever-changing.

Writing instructors are, at best, gardeners. We toil. We sweat. But little by little, we can improve our gardens. We can design structures that allow all to flourish. We can implement processes that provide individual and personal nourishment. We can ensure that each individual is supported so they may reach their true growth potential. And it is good to know that this solitary work is not done alone, even when we feel like we work and write in solitude.

Scott Bayer, English teacher, instructional coach,
keynote speaker, and cofounder of #THEBOOKCHAT
June 2023

Acknowledgments

This is my third book with Norton, and it has been a wonderful journey. Many thanks to all team members past and present who have made my books possible: Mariah Eppes, Olivia Guarnieri, Emma Paolini, Meredith John, Natalie Argentina, Kevin Olsen, and Jamie Vincent. Most of all, heartfelt gratitude to my editor, Carol Chambers Collins. I'm so honored to have worked with you.

To my teacher contributors: Benson Voss, Kristen Engle, Adria Hoffman, Steve McMahon, and James Schafer. Your collaboration and expertise made this book a true joy to write. Thank you for sharing creative and practical instructional strategies that work so well in classrooms across content areas.

To Scott Bayer, who has such a profound passion for facilitating meaningful instruction for all students, I am so touched that you took the time to write a beautiful foreword that embraces the spirit of this book.

Many thanks to education friends both near and far who have helped me on this journey, especially Jon Bergmann, Nicholas Emmanuele, Daryl Howard, Joe Pizzo, Alex Shevrin Venet, and Brett Vogelsinger. I'm also incredibly lucky to work with a dream team in my district that supports me and challenges my thinking in all the best ways.

In the conclusion of this book, I write about the influence my beloved father had on my career. To Daddy: I know you're out there somewhere being proud. I miss you so much, and I love you.

To my mother, thank you for getting me through those rough preteen days when I cried every day after school, and in more recent times, for reminding me to share what I write with you. It means a lot that you never want to miss a single word.

My biggest cheerleaders are my children, whose unwavering belief in my work inspires me daily. Kiddos, thanks for being so great about my being a general pain in the you-know-what when I write. Believe me, I know not every mother has such a fantastic crew. Koby, your side job as my tech expert and skillful creator of all publicity is something I will always need, so don't go far. Ayla, you always tell me that I'm doing this whole mothering and adulting thing right, which is beyond reassuring and so kind. Dalya, you never let me get too serious and remind me to take frequent writing breaks to get snacks or receive hugs. It helps, I promise!

And to Kenny, who brings me coffee every single day (the ultimate gesture of romance) and is never surprised when another book or article is accepted for publication because he believes in me that much—you make everything better, all the time. Thanks for managing everyone's extracurricular schedules, appointments, and mealtimes so that I could get things done and have time for little sanity breaks. Love you.

Introduction:
The Journey to Identity

This book is part of a long string of happy surprises.

Like many people who get into teaching, it was not my intention to stay in the classroom for long. In the first few years of my career, I lived in Washington, D.C., where no matter how much anyone tries to avoid politics, it had a way of always being front and center during social interactions. With that pervasive influence, I pursued a graduate degree in education policy at The George Washington University in the evenings, with a full-time course load, while working in a public high school all day in both my first and second years of teaching. The resultant exhaustion might not have looked like a traditional recipe for success, but I made it to year three of teaching and decided to remain in the classroom for a few more years before heading into the policy sector.

And then, something unpredictable happened. Feeling the need to work with a wider range of students, I transferred to a school with a much larger percentage of what we in education call a "highly impacted" population. I began working with teenagers who had different life experiences to pull from than mine, and suddenly, I was hooked on teaching. The years began to slip by, one after another, and it took some self-awareness to realize that Plan A (i.e., to quit and head toward Capitol Hill) was no

longer what I wanted. Being in a classroom with kids every day was a far
more appealing option.

Somewhere in the middle of this time, I started experimenting with
the student-centered methods that became the groundwork for the "hover-
free" teaching philosophy outlined in my first book, *Teach More, Hover
Less*. For nearly twenty years, I remained in the classroom to work with
kids and figure out how to empower them to not only make meaning of
the content on their own terms, but to also feel secure in their capacity
as learners. No matter how confident the many students I worked with
seemed to be, or how much I tried to intuit what everyone needed, nearly
every child who came through my classroom had plenty of self-doubt
about their academic worth in at least one content area, if not more.

When my career took me into school leadership and provided insight
for my second book, *Lead Like a Teacher*, I continued to focus on the role
instructional methodology plays in nearly every aspect of how teaching and leading provides a functional space for kids to flourish—or not.
Then, I took on a role as a district-level specialist, which provided a view
into classrooms in multiple schools and gave me a new vantage point to
observe how students, both vocally and silently, communicate their feelings about the learning opportunities and environment in front of them.

And then—the pandemic hit. While the consequences and traumatic
results of what began in 2020 continue to reverberate in school buildings
everywhere, one continuing question teachers face is how to help this
generation of children. Across the board, students have changed, and not
just in terms of learning disruption. They have become more isolated, less
socially nimble, more insecure, more uncertain. In our secondary schools,
preteens and teens might be openly angry or hostile, or they may simply
be confused. So much of the stability they experienced earlier in their
young lives has crumbled around them, and even as the adults around
them try to recover, our continuous stumbling has not inspired much
confidence in the observant eyes of kids around us.

Into this mix comes the complexity of identity. When students returned
for in-person learning in what so many teachers look at as a disastrous
year in 2021, much of the advice and counsel we received was to prioritize social–emotional learning (SEL) above all other instructional needs.
Everyone had been through too much, and we needed to recalibrate and

figure out where students were coming from on a more personal level before diving headlong into instruction.

As everyone knows by now, there was more disruption to come, and homing in on SEL (then and now a highly necessary area of focus) was not enough to mitigate the damage of another year of further disrupted instruction. Through this instability, students continued to feel untethered, and their sense of their own learning capacity likely went down. Time and research will tell a more concrete story, one that links correlations to their proper root causations.

While my first two books reflect the journey I took from teacher to leader, this one represents the days and years to come for all of us who are on this path in education together. We do not know what lies ahead, and we cannot reassure the students we care so much about that their world will right itself. Instead, we must thoughtfully serve the children with whom we work, in the best way we can, no matter what conditions swirl around us. To do that, empowering students to feel a sense of worth in their own ability not just in school but also in the lives they will go on to lead becomes infinitely more crucial.

Teachers hope that students will be good people, and we do our best to make classrooms pleasant and productive places to learn. Now more than ever, kids need their teachers to be a force for sanity and stability. This truth is self-evident. However, there is another need that students cry out for, one they may not be able to identify without help: to be seen as legitimate, valuable contributors to the world around them. Without teachers who validate their ideas and worth in the classroom and beyond, students will not reach their full potential.

This book is about tearing down the destructive mythology around deficit thinking by using writing instruction—one of the biggest areas of conflict for students who think they are "bad" at something—as an access point for achievement. The strategies and tools that are sprinkled liberally throughout these chapters may begin with writing, but do not be fooled into thinking that this book is only for English teachers. Just about every activity contained in this text can be applied to multiple secondary content areas. As a special bonus, at the close of several chapters, teachers from a variety of subjects share their tried-and-true strategies for building academic identity.

To understand what the phrase "academic identity" means and how the idea came about, coming to a mutual understanding of why establishing teacher-student rapport (while still highly important) is not the be-all-end-all panacea for fixing the damage that has been wrought over the past three or so years of pandemic-era disruption is important. By exploring deeper connections and their power to transform the student experience, perhaps everyone can get a little closer to tearing down the systems that do not work, making way for new progress and opportunity.

Defining Academic Identity

In the struggle to give this book a title that would clearly communicate its purpose, I waffled over including the term "academic identity" somewhere on the cover, eventually opting to omit the phrase around which this book is centered and go with language that requires less initial explanation. Before going any further, however, let's pause to establish the working definition of what it means to talk about students having an "academic identity."

When *Teach More, Hover Less* was newly out, I had a discussion with a colleague about the second stage of "hover-free" teaching, which is about reframing relationships. We delved into a teaching stereotype that is fairly pervasive, which is that of the "popular" or "cool" teacher. This individual is nearly universally well-liked; students love hanging out with this teacher at lunch or after school; and kids actively try to "get into" this person's class, anticipating a special experience.

Invariably, a smaller percentage of students who are initially excited to learn with this teacher wind up feeling disappointed. Their peers might be connecting with this teacher, but this less enchanted group feels uncomfortable in the class. For one reason or another, the relationship doesn't click and the students who are not as fond of this popular teacher are left to wonder: *What's wrong with me?*

At one point, most of us have probably experienced this discomfort in a classroom. I vividly remember not jelling with a widely beloved high school teacher who nearly everyone else raved about. When I was in his classroom, I felt invisible. He bantered with most of the other kids and seemed to connect with them, and for reasons that must have amounted to personal chemistry, I never had the same experience. His eyes would simply roam right over me and find a different student to engage with. At that age, I blamed myself for this consistent non-interaction. After all, everyone else seemed to do just fine.

Years later, I had the revelation that led to the second stage of "hover-free" teaching and that also guides this book. When students do not feel safe to express their ideas in a classroom, it is the direct result of how the teacher designs interaction. The power of personal rapport cannot be understated in student learning; however, that is not the final piece of the puzzle in empowering student voice and achievement. There is one more thing that has to happen for most children to perform at maximum capacity: they must have clear evidence that their teachers believe in their ability to make valuable contributions to learning.

The resultant idea of "academic identity" is central to this book. For the purpose of establishing a common understanding, here is a definition of the term:

> ACADEMIC IDENTITY: A strong intrinsic sense of value
> in one's own capacity to make profound contributions
> to scholarship in classroom settings and beyond.

The above definition is intentional in its application not just to school settings, but also to what students take away with them once they leave classrooms and enter the next phase of their lives. While the objective of life beyond school may seem outside the scope of practice for teachers, one of our implicit jobs is to give students skills that transfer past the limited time that they inhabit our classes.

At the start of this chapter, I shared that this book holds a special place in my heart, and it also mirrors my professional journey. As a curriculum specialist in secondary English Language Arts and literacy who found my way back to the power of writing after working with students in all grade levels and content areas, I can affirm that there is no way to understate the importance of allowing students to express themselves in safe zones, which often happens through the written medium in every single secondary subject.

How, then, to achieve the goal of building academic identity for all students, not just the ones who happen to have a personal affinity for the teacher in front of them? The answer begins with effective professional development. When that phrase is uttered in school hallways, teachers sometimes cringe as they envision a team of outside experts delivering directives via PowerPoint. Instead, in the spirit of affirming that the truest instructional experts are the people who occupy classrooms each day, let us instead consider how teachers and students collaborate with school leaders to establish academic identity within all classrooms.

The Best Professional Development

Of the many nuggets of wisdom educators share, one apt idea is that the best available professional development resource is the teacher down the hall. It is not only practical to turn to colleagues in proximity for thought partnership; it is also professionally satisfying to discuss mutual needs, challenges, or triumphs that occur in the natural course of daily instruction.

While a book cannot replicate the experience of chatting with someone down the hall, it can provide fodder for discussion and collaboration. From *Teach More, Hover Less* to *Lead Like a Teacher* to this new offering, my goal has remained the same: prioritize practical strategies for application. The number of figures, strategies, and tools shared in the next several chapters are plentiful and span multiple areas of need across secondary subject areas. When time is less plentiful than any teacher would like (which is the norm), it is not just possible, but recommended that readers flip through the pages, find any strategies that look relevant, and apply them immediately to classroom practice, either as-is or with any adjustments that best suit the needs of students.

The term "professional development" has gotten a bad rap over the past several years, sometimes deservedly so. My second book, *Lead Like a Teacher*, outlines the many reasons that training sessions go awry, from tone-deaf content to inept delivery. One obvious way to make professional development useful is to listen to teachers when they express what they need, but an even more powerful solution is for teachers themselves to lead one another in learning for growth. The reason that colleagues down the hall are the best professional developers is because they are *there*. In classrooms. With kids. There is no greater source for instructional expertise. That is why, throughout this book, teachers across content areas share their most effective strategies for building student academic identity in subjects like math, physics, physical education, and music.

To honor the collectivist approach this book recommends, consider sharing the tools and strategies not just with the teacher down the hall, but also with school leaders and with students. To empower all members of a school community, teachers must continue to find value in all voices, even or perhaps especially the ones we do not agree with. Ideally, administrators will be inspired by the benefits that academic identity confers onto students and share what they learn with school leaders in other locations. Maybe students will take their newfound sense of confidence and encourage classmates or friends to believe in their ability to make progress. The possibilities are limitless when teachers take the time to nurture not just a teaching friend, but also multitudes of others as we shatter damaging myths about student capacity and replace them with new stories.

Shattering the Myth

Bianca is terrified.

In the first month of school, she has managed to fly under the radar in nearly all her classes, as usual. She sits somewhere in the middle of the room, answering questions in a soft voice when called upon, which happens rarely. Long ago, Bianca learned not to make eye contact with teachers because 95 percent of the time, not looking up means their eyes wander right over her to focus on another student.

Much to her dismay, today is different. On Bianca's way out of social studies yesterday, Mr. Parsons stopped her at the doorway. "Tomorrow we're sharing our current events projects," he said, "and I'd like for you to share yours."

Bianca turned red. "M-me?" she stuttered, her heart racing.

Mr. Parsons seemed to realize she was afraid and hastened to reassure her. "I'm asking you to share for a reason," he said. "Your project on what's happening in Ukraine was so insightful. Do you have a personal interest in the topic?"

"My grandfather was from Kyiv," Bianca shared, her voice barely audible.

"Wow, that's amazing. So, you have that connection, and you also went really thoroughly into many of the deeper points of cultural dissonance between people in Ukraine and Russia. It would be so cool to hear you talk about it."

Just wanting to get out of there, Bianca nodded. "Okay."

Now, she's kicking herself for agreeing to share her project with the class. Why didn't she find an excuse to say no? She has been sitting in a room with these kids for a month, and while they're not an unfriendly group, Bianca hasn't really talked to any of them. Mr. Parsons must be blind, or he would have noticed that nobody ever talks to her or seems to even realize that she's there.

As class begins, Bianca takes out her materials, hoping against hope that Mr. Parsons has either forgotten about the whole thing or that he runs out of time. That hope is quickly dashed when he starts the class by announcing, "After our activator, we'll be looking more in depth at two current events projects from your classmates. Bianca and Gary will both share their work."

Oh no, Bianca thinks, sinking down in her seat as several sets of eyes swivel toward her in undisguised surprise. *What have I gotten myself into?*

When the time comes for Bianca to share, she somehow makes it to the front of the room. On the screen behind her, Mr. Parsons has her slides ready to go. As she starts, her voice is soft. "I wanted to focus on the war in Ukraine for two reasons," she says. "The first is, my grandfather's family was from Ukraine, and I've grown up hearing a lot about the culture since he lives with us. The second is that everyone paid attention to the war in the beginning, but now it seems like it's been forgotten with everything else happening in the world. So, this project is my way of giving everybody what my mom would call a 'friendly' reminder."

From the middle of the room, a boy pipes up. "Adults always say that, and then you *know* it's not so friendly."

Everyone laughs, and Bianca realizes they're laughing with her, not at her. She relaxes another fraction, just enough to go into her next slide and become immersed in the story she is telling. As she delves into how the history of the two countries has led to the current conflict, she barely notices her classmates anymore. Her voice becomes louder, stronger, and more expressive.

When Bianca reaches the end of her slides, nobody is more surprised than she is that the dreaded presentation is over. In fact, several hands shoot up into the air. Mr. Parsons checks in with Bianca. "Feel like answering some questions?"

She nods and is pleased that she not only gets insightful questions from classmates she normally doesn't talk to, but that she also knows the answers. A few students aren't even asking questions, but instead tell her how interesting her presentation was, how much they learned, and that they appreciate getting a peer's perspective on headlines their eyes usually just skim over. When Bianca sits down to a generous amount of applause, there is a warm feeling in her she did not expect, and her cheeks burn with pride instead of embarrassment.

"Before we hear from Gary, I want to thank Bianca for sharing her project," Mr. Parsons says. "In particular, the nuance she presented in the relationship between two countries that share so many cultural experiences and history was highly mature in its analysis. When two groups are at war, we're often tempted to think in solid dichotomies, or by pitting them in shallow ways against each other. It's always more subtle, and Bianca's project captured that."

As the class moves on and Gary gets up to make his presentation, Bianca feels both relieved and inspired. The time that Mr. Parsons took to explain why he appreciated her project has helped her to feel seen, and the presentation went better than she ever could have dreamed. Her ideas always make sense in her own head, but it's so good to know that other people might see the same value in her that she has always hoped lies somewhere beneath the surface.

But now, Gary is up at the front, and Bianca wants to give him the same respect and attention that others gave her just a few minutes ago. Maybe she will hear something new and be able to contribute an encouraging word to her classmate when his presentation concludes. She knows her ideas are worth something, and she will spend the rest of this year in Mr. Parson's class proving herself each day.

WRITING THEIR FUTURE SELVES

Rejecting the Myth of the Bad Writer

Writing Insecurity

"I'm a bad writer." "I need more time." "I'm just warning you, this is terrible."

Welcome to what I call "The Disclaimer." Teachers of writing are familiar with what most students do before they share their work with anyone. For years, I watched even the most confident writers fall prey to The Disclaimer. It made an appearance no matter the situation—whether students were being asked to share their pieces, whether they volunteered unasked, whether they felt good about what they'd created or not.

When I think about The Disclaimer, a scene from earlier in my teaching career comes to mind. It is October 31st, and my students have been working on a writing challenge for the past month as they read snippets of Mary Shelley, Octavia Butler, Edgar Allan Poe, and Stephen King: Write something scary. The prospect of trying to terrify their peers is intimidating, and some students have fallen back on humor, writing so-called "scary" stories about common teenage afflictions like breaking out in acne or applying to college. Those who have taken the task in earnest are understandably more nervous as the day arrives to share their writing. What if their work fails to elicit the ideal response?

I try to be reassuring as the anticipatory buzz intennifirs. "Frightening another person is incredibly difficult to do," I say. "When we write, we aim to elicit some kind of emotional response, and we also want readers to turn the page. If we accomplish that, we've already made a lot of progress. Now, do we have some volunteers who are ready to share?"

The response is predictable. The same four students who always ask to go first and who are already at the edge of their seats with excitement shoot their hands straight into the air. Other students sit back, relieved. While the expectation is that most of the class will read their work aloud or pass their papers around to read silently, those who feel more hesitant have been granted a temporary reprieve. Not surprisingly, the students who volunteer first are popular, well-liked, vocal, and frequent class contributors. Three are male. Also not surprisingly, these four students do not necessarily consider themselves to be future writers, nor are they the hardest working individuals in the class. Some of the more skillful writers, the ones who produce the response I identified as ideal, will never willingly put their writing into the hands of others in the class until specifically forced to do so. When that happens and their work is well-received and appreciated, their confidence increases. When it is met with a less overtly approving response, they remain shut into themselves.

For the next hour, students share their scary stories. After the first eager beavers have duly gone and received verbal praise or feedback, it is harder to convince more reticent students to come to the front of the room and read aloud. Often, I accidentally tune out during the less engaging presenters or less skillful content, but now and then, I perk up when I hear something more exciting. The class mirrors my behavior, reacting verbally to what they perceive as excellent and even shrieking when frightened, or by applauding a little more loudly at the conclusion of the presentation. When students get this enthusiastic response, they glow. When they do not, they smile at the polite applause and return to their seats, privately disappointed. The torturous thoughts are written across their faces: *I was right. I'm a bad writer.*

No matter how each student feels at the end of reading aloud, however, nearly all begin the same way. Before they dive in, they say something along the lines of, "Sorry, guys. This isn't that good. I wrote it really fast, and I couldn't figure out the ending. Anyway, yeah. Sorry."

As much as I might reassure students and try to stop them from sharing The Disclaimer, they will never be able to feel comfortable unless the fundamental issue—writing insecurity—is dealt with more effectively for *all* members of the classroom community. Even if I am caring and encouraging and believe in my students, I will remain truly frustrated that more students are not volunteering to share their stories. I am excited at the quality of the work students produce and their enthusiasm for the class, but want everyone to feel that same sense of productive anticipation. How can I keep what works, but fix what is clearly broken?

In earlier grades, students exhibit more faith in their own writing skills, but there is a sharp drop-off in their self-perception and engagement after the elementary years. As a 2015 Gallup Poll reveals, students move from about 75% engagement in fifth grade to 34% in the twelfth, bottoming out at a low 32% their junior year of high school (Brenneman, 2016). Around the same time that children begin to grow more reticent about their own skills, accountability measures ramp up as they enter the secondary grades. Suddenly, everything "counts" toward the ever-nearer destinations of college and career. Teachers are more prone to using phrases like "in the real world," or "in college, professors expect" in reference to the work students produce, often when it fails to meet a desired standard. Assessments also become more high stakes, as tests like the SAT and Advanced Placement exams pave the way for college admissions and credit. The more students hear about what they need to do to be successful adults, the more intimidated many become. Depending on endless combinations of factors that range anywhere from individual personality traits to the support parents are equipped to provide at home, the way students respond to this sort of extrinsic motivation often runs counter to what adults expect. Rather than accomplish the objective of ensuring that students understand the gravity of their education and buckle down, threatening them with what might happen if they are unsuccessful can stymie growth.

With writing, this problem is magnified because of the personal risk that is associated with sharing what we create. Writing is an expression of the self, which connects directly to how we expose our inner realities to the outside world, no matter how old or successful we become. I am a middle-aged professional writer with years of experience and documented recognized in my field of expertise. However, whenever my work is rejected (a frequent experience for almost every writer on the planet), my first reaction is nearly always: *I'm not good enough.* If I respond that way, imagine how students feel when they take the significant risk of putting their work out into the classroom for all to see. Then, intensify that feeling to account not just for youth, emotional response, and inexperience, but also for a marginalized sense of self. Is it any wonder that kids whose voices may have been stifled elsewhere do not feel comfortable sharing their writing with others? Too many learning environments are simply not safe enough, nor are they set up to become so.

The only way to shift an outdated status quo is to recognize that the problem of inaccessible writing instruction is real, develop new structures and processes that redesign current norms, and continue course-correcting whatever needs to be tweaked. To begin engaging students in writing instruction that includes a more affirming and accessible teaching lens, teachers must first actively interrupt the myth students hold that they are "bad" writers.

Celebrating Individual and Collective Writing Voice

How students perceive themselves as writers cannot be underestimated or brushed aside. America is a notoriously individualistic society, and that has never been truer in our current reality. As educators who follow the increasing regression of student achievement data may already realize, the vision of students working in bubbles to strive hard and reach success can be a rigged game. Our education system is not set up for all students to succeed, and that is largely due to our inability to see past the systems that no longer hold the same effectiveness they did even just a few years ago. Unraveling our beliefs about self-reliance is key to ensuring that we apply a more culturally responsive and more inclusive lens to building student identity beyond the classroom.

In *Culturally Responsive Teaching and the Brain*, implicit bias expert Zaretta Hammond (2015) discusses the cultural archetypes of collectivism and individualism, and how they influence the way we think. Hammond observes that while Americans are highly individualistic to the point of that lens dominating our culture, other societies (African

American, Latino, Pacific Islander, and Native American) are collectivist (p. 25). When these conflicting cultural norms enter a classroom setting, the dissonance that results can be difficult to overcome.

With writing instruction, the expectations around communication become even more complex when we consider differences in cultural expectation. As Hammond points out: "Some cultures have relied on the spoken word rather than the written word to convey, preserve, and reproduce knowledge from generation to generation" (p. 28). An emphasis on oral versus written tradition can alter the way a child is taught to process ideas and share them. If that child then enters a classroom and learns that there is only one so-called "legitimate" way to communicate ideas (i.e., through writing), and that the written word is grounded in formulaic structures that are embraced by academia while the oral tradition is disregarded, they may already feel a decrease in self-worth.

Putting these ideas together, the point is not to stop teaching various forms of academic writing, nor is it to replace writing with oral communication. However, if teachers fail to consider the advantages around collectivist classroom norms, they will continue to encounter many students who feel isolated in their perceived inability to increase achievement. In other words, writing instruction cannot occur in individual bubbles, nor should it be any kind of competitive endeavor. By embracing ideas over formatting, student voice can shine through more naturally in speaking *and* in writing, which are two of the four needed language domains for all learners (the other two being reading and listening).

What does a classroom look like when it prioritizes the whole over the one, and when it embraces the role of speaking as a pathway to better writing? Table 1.1 shares a possible classroom setup for any given week.

In a model like the one featured in Table 1.1, the content of the class shifts, while the way the teacher designs instruction follows a specific progression that allows students to move through each day with a clear understanding of their larger learning target. Early in the week, the teacher provides direct instruction to the large group, sharing content or practical expertise to set everyone up for the productive days ahead. Then, two days a week are set aside (in this case, Tuesday and Thursday) for students to work more independently on their writing or engage in stations with other possible classroom activities, such as reading assignments, shorter tasks

TABLE 1.1

Day	Structure
Monday	WHOLE GROUP INSTRUCTION • Teacher-led • Introduce new concepts or ideas • Share logistical details for the upcoming week
Tuesday	WRITING TIME • Drafting • Peer editing or consulting • Teacher feedback (conferencing) • Stations as applicable
Wednesday	CHECK-IN • Small groups or whole class • Formative assessment • Voice feedback
Thursday	WRITING TIME • Course-correction from feedback on feedback • Drafting • Peer editing or consulting • Teacher feedback (conferencing) • Stations as applicable
Friday	FUN FRIDAY! • Writing game or student-led writing activity • Share and/or discuss writing products • Celebrate successes of the past week

or smaller group collaboration. Since it is wise to check the temperature of how each week progresses, there is a designated midweek check-in day, during which the teacher has the opportunity to gather information about how students are faring through methods such as quick formative assessment or voice-driven feedback. This time is ideal to gather student input that helps us determine whether the instructional plan for the week is working as anticipated, what roadblocks may be interfering with success, and how to tweak the remainder of the week to meet student needs. Once teachers have looked through what students share, following a "feedback on feedback" protocol in which we transparently tell the class what is changing (and what must remain the same) as a result of their ideas is important for fostering a sense of trust. Finally, the schedule features a "Fun Friday," which is a day devoted to extracting more joy from the writing process. An illustration of such a day is located a little later in this chapter.

As Table 1.1 demonstrates, a classroom model that allows for a balance between teacher-directed instruction and student-centered activity can be far more culturally responsive because of its inherent value of multiple perspectives, as opposed to a traditional writing classroom in which the teacher spends each day modeling a desired product, method or format before students attempt to replicate what has been demonstrated. By switching up the way students approach learning in a way that also allows teachers to plan ahead, the result is a flexible, dynamic classroom that recognizes the importance of every individual in the room.

Resistance to a structure like the one featured in Table 1.1 is that while it may be engaging to teach a class in this way, some people perceive the result to be teachers lowering rigor or expectations. However, rigor is grounded less in how a class is organized or how difficult it is believed to be and more in what high expectations for students look like. For example, when we make a task difficult, that does not mean it is more rigorous; it often means that the assignment is badly constructed. Think about a test that many students fail. Is that because the test is rigorous, or is the assessment itself at fault? Either is possible. With complexity of course materials and assignments, the rigor of expectation is around how teachers hold students accountable for meeting grade-level standards through assignments that are aligned to the appropriate age and stage. Building teacher capacity and awareness around designing instruction to meet the correct expectations is vital to student growth, and it also helps to place conversations about rigor in their proper place. How we structure our classes does not increase or decrease academic rigor; it is the teaching and learning itself that must be held up to the light.

A second point of resistance for a structure like the one featured in Table 1.1 is that when teachers plan for student engagement by varying the way a class is organized each day, that makes their jobs harder because they have to do more work. In *Teach More, Hover Less* (2022), my guide to "hover-free" teaching that reduces micromanagement in the secondary classroom, I explain that the act of preparing instruction with the understanding that the plan is slightly subject to change simply acknowledges reality. After all, even in the most teacher-driven classrooms, things do not go as expected. In a student-centered classroom, teachers have more freedom during instruction to be agile. As I write in Chapter 3 of the book, "Adjusting our classroom approach to focus on overarching goals with flexible means of achieving outcomes may include more forethought in the planning stages of teaching, but it frees up our time during class so that more engaging instruction is possible" (p. 46).

In addition, the question is not whether adding a structure that is more student-centered creates more work, but rather where existing work goes. When teachers plan without bringing student feedback into the mix, they often have to go back and reteach concepts that did not take the first time. Therefore, what seems to be less time-consuming actually eats up more bandwidth, and teachers may end up being rushed to complete a curriculum progression when they feel the need to repeat instruction.

After the first year of the COVID-19 pandemic resulted in the coinage of the controversial phrase "learning loss," educators debated about the best methods for reassimilating students into school buildings and catching them up on any missed curricular content. What many teachers and administrators discovered was that going backward into previous grade levels to remediate supposedly "lost" content was not as effective an approach as what is known as "learning acceleration," which (confusing terminology aside) is defined as engaging in good first instruction with students at their expected level of content entry. In the *Atlantic* article "Our Kids Are Not Broken" by teacher and writer Ron Berger (2021), Berger shares the research findings of mathematician Phillip Uri Treisman, who has spent his career examining why fewer Black and Latino students receive higher degrees in mathematics. Treisman "took a novel approach to this problem that has shifted thinking nationally. His research revealed that when students interested in pursuing mathematics were assigned remedial work, it was essentially a dead end for those students' future in math." As Berger himself seconds:

> *If districts focus too much on remediating "learning loss"—*
> *holding kids back a grade, categorizing students according to*
> *their deficits, and centering lesson plans on catch-up work—*
> *the students who have experienced the most trauma and*

disconnection during the pandemic may be assigned to the lowest level and most stigmatized groups. They will be viewed as deficient, and the inequities in place before and during the pandemic will be further amplified. Children, having been told that they are behind, will internalize the story of their loss.

The connections among ideas around learning loss, accessible writing instruction, and building student identity to combat the myth of "bad" writing (i.e., students' own sense of incapacity) are intricately woven into the fabric of how we set up classrooms for better results. Providing better structures for student voice is key, which is why a more dynamic classroom model like the one featured in Table 1.1 is so important to understanding each student we encounter. In addition, the "Fun Friday" concept provided in Table 1.1 is a way to increase engagement while still focusing on building writing skills.

To provide a deeper illustration of how a "Fun Friday" might work for writing instruction, picture an eighth-grade language arts classroom on a dreary winter afternoon. Students have been working hard all week on an essay that asks them to compare and contrast the determination of two characters from separate books and argue which character is the most effective at getting what they want. Students have had much of the week to draft their thoughts, work with the teacher, and collaborate with peers. With all the headway everyone has made, the teacher is more than ready to let students engage in a "Fun Friday" writing game.

The activity she selects is called The Magic Box. Students are directed to write a short synopsis of a story idea on a sheet of scrap paper. The only rule is that the synopsis has to include both a main character and some kind of conflict. Once that is done, students fold up their papers and place them into a box (a bucket, hat, or bin also works, but this teacher uses a beautifully decorated cardboard shoe box) that is sitting at the front of the room.

When students have all placed their papers into the box, the teacher shuffles the scraps around by placing the lid on top and shaking the box. Then, she steps back and holds her hands up. "Time to choose!"

Some students rush directly to the front, excited to pick out their story idea. Others wait until the crowd clears, knowing there will be a paper scrap for them regardless of how quickly they move.

When students are back at their desks, they open up the folded papers and read. Some are audibly excited to see the synopsis they pulled at random ("This is an awesome idea!") while others groan ("How am I supposed to write this? I don't get it!"). Many students read quietly and begin to think about what to write, opening up their notebooks to a fresh page. As this happens, the teacher walks around, smiling and offering encouragement as well as refusing any requests to trade: "You get what you get and you might be upset, but write. You can do this."

For about 20 minutes, the room is silent except for the sound of pens or pencils scratching on paper and the occasional laugh or sigh. The teacher circulates, remaining as unobtrusive as possible while glancing at some of the story synopses that lie open on desks. When the time draws to a close for writing, she gives them a two-minute warning. "Remember," she says, "the goal is not to finish the story. The goal is to create something that feels like it has potential."

As students prepare to share what they have written, the teacher gives them two options. The first is to volunteer to share the story, and the second is to ask for whoever built out their synopsis to share. Either way, the process is that students read the story first, and after the class has reacted, they share the synopsis they were given as a point of comparison.

Some of the students are called on randomly because of a classmate's wish to hear their synopsis come to life, while others choose to read their work aloud. Either way, the protocols are the same. At the close of the story, the class is asked to provide each writer with a "warm fuzzy," which is a series of compliments about the elements of the story they enjoyed. Students are also encouraged to ask questions. More often than not, the writer of the synopsis expresses admiration for the person who brought the frame of their idea into greater detail and focus.

The role of a "Fun Friday" in creating a collaborative classroom that prioritizes the collective over the individual and opens access and opportunity for multiple voices to be heard cannot be underestimated. Naysayers may argue that games or activities that are designed for student engagement hold less academic value, but that argument is flawed. Rigorous instruction is grounded in critical thinking and in the cognitive flexibility to work through challenging tasks. When students participate in activities like The Magic Box, they draw from a variety of necessary skills: problem-solving (especially those who are flummoxed by what to do with the synopsis), application of ideas, clear communication, and the ability to place themselves in the perspectives of others. Also not to be discounted, the mere act of writing more produces heightened capacity. The more we read, the better readers we become, and the same holds true of writing. Just as important, the access of such an activity for all students in the classroom increases the opportunity to hear multiple voices in a safe learning space. Suddenly, something that seems like simple fun or a game becomes much more substantial, underscoring the deeper purpose behind a "Fun Friday" routine.

Nurturing the way each individual student voice contributes to the collective benefit of our classrooms is complex work, but teachers who recognize the power of opening up more rigid structures to make way for flexible practice are rewarded with a classroom that exhibits a more visible approach to building student identity.

Interrupting the Myth

One day in the middle of a semester, a new student transferred from another district and entered my English class. Yasmin's demeanor was not open or friendly. Instead, she seemed drawn into herself. Her clothing was dark, a chain dangled from her belt and into the pocket of her ripped jeans, and her arms were covered in tattoos. Underneath a large pair of glasses and a knit cap, her face was studded with nose, lip, and brow rings. She did not meet my eyes as I asked her some questions about what she liked to read and write, which school she had come from, and how I could help her get up to speed in a way that wouldn't be too overwhelming. She was polite and her voice was soft, but she exhibited no enthusiasm as she sat down.

Partway through class, I noticed that her head was bent to focus on a point beneath the desk. That typically meant that someone was stealthily using a phone, so I circled around behind Yasmin to see better. To my surprise, she was writing in a composition notebook, her pen moving with fast and vigorous strokes. The rest of the class was working on a project, but I did not want to interrupt my new pupil. Why would I want to stop her when inspiration seemed to have struck?

As the class period ended and students began to pack up their

In hanging, I walked over to her. "I hope you don't mind my asking, but I noticed that you were writing. Is that something your writing?"

She shrugged. "I guess."

Her manner was not encouraging, but I pressed on. "Is it mainly just your own stuff you enjoy writing, or do you also like what teachers ask you to do?"

"Mainly my own. I mean, I don't hate the other writing, but it's usually kind of boring."

I nodded. "It can be. Maybe you'll share something you do with me sometime?"

"Maybe." I could tell she thought that would never happen.

Over the next couple of weeks, I worked on building a relationship with Yasmin that focused on her capability as a learner. She sent a very clear message that she guarded her personal privacy, so I was careful not to intrude into that aspect of her life. Instead, we talked about the class project she was working on, how to get her caught up with various assignments, and what she read or wrote in her previous school. She always did what I asked, was cooperative if not effusive, and participated in collaborative activities. She also made gradual progress with getting to know her classmates, and I even saw her joking around with the students in her table group now and then.

About two months into her time in my class, I assigned a piece that asked students to imitate the style of one of the writers whose short stories we were reading. Yasmin chose to give Edith Wharton a try. The class had recently read "Roman Fever," and the unbelievable twist at the end of the story left many students gasping or shaking their heads in disbelief. Yasmin had a slightly different reaction. As she read Wharton's closing words, her eyes widened and scrawled something on her copy of the story. When I walked by, I saw that she had written, *How did she do that?*

Yasmin was clearly taken not just with what Wharton had done, but also *how* she had accomplished such a skillful turnaround in the final three words of her story. A door to a different way of structuring a short story suddenly opened, and I saw Yasmin take out her notebook and begin sketching out ideas for her style imitation project with new inspiration.

When the projects were complete, I was in for yet another surprise. Before class began, Yasmin walked up to me and asked, "Are we sharing today?"

"We are," I said. "I'm pretty excited to see what everyone did."

She looked straight at me. "Can I share mine first? I know you like to call on people randomly, but I'm nervous. It would help to do it before I talk myself out of it."

I tried not to jump up and down as I agreed. Her willingness to put herself out there was new, and I wanted to make sure she had no reason to regret it. When it was time to share, she went to the front of the room with her stapled pages in front of her, and I held my breath.

What followed was a detailed, dramatic story about a family that was just as scandalous (if not more) as any characters Edith Wharton had ever created. As one deeply rooted family secret after another was exposed, the class began to move beyond quick intakes of breath and whispered "ohmigods." Their reactions grew louder and more emphatic, and with this gradual crescendo, Yasmin's soft voice became stronger. The story was raw, and it had plenty of errors in both grammar and mechanics. Those mistakes would be easy to fix, but the fact was, Yasmin had power that many writers envy. She knew how to captivate an audience with a series of shockers and plot twists.

While I wanted to congratulate Yasmin right away on her success, I waited and watched as classmates approached her to share their accolades. Suddenly, she was part of the community in a new way, and her wider smile told me everything about how lonely she might have been, and how happy she was now.

As class ended, I called Yasmin up to my desk. "That was a pretty incredible story," I said. "How did you think of that?"

She looked down, suddenly back to being reticent. "I didn't, really. It's not as good as everyone thinks."

I shook my head. "That's not true. It is very good. But why do you think it's not?"

"Because," she said, her face growing red. "It's all true."

Suddenly, a lot clicked into place. Yasmin, lover of the plot twist, had dropped yet another bomb. This sordid family tale we had just heard full of moments that seemed pulled right out of a daytime soap opera was not the work of her imagination—it was real. No wonder she was so guarded, so self-protective. She had been through more than any person should be, and at such a young age.

At that moment, I felt ashamed. I should have somehow realized that her inspiration came from somewhere beyond her imagination, and I know that maintaining Yasmin's trust was the highest priority given her vulnerability and her history. I told her, "I can't tell you how much I appreciate that you feel comfortable sharing your story with me and the class. And you should know that fiction writers draw from the truth all the time, which is exactly what you did. It doesn't make your writing any less important or legitimate."

Yasmin nodded, but I wasn't entirely convinced that she believed me. While making a mental note to check on her physical and emotional well-being with her school counselor, I also had to be sure that Yasmin felt intellectually safe in my class. What could I do to help her understand that even if she felt insecure about some aspects of writing, her work held value?

Convincing students that their work is better than they think is a difficult task, one that begins with altering our language around writing. Table 1.2 shares some commonly held student thoughts about their "bad" writing capabilities in the left-hand column and provides responses that "flip" the myth to reality so that teachers can respond productively when kids express a lack of belief in themselves.

TABLE 1.2

The Myth	The Reality
I'm a terrible writer. Nothing ever turns out the way I want it to.	You have so many valuable ideas to share.
I never learned grammar, so none of my thoughts make sense.	Grammar is just one aspect of writing, and we can learn more about how to improve.
I tried to write this, but it didn't work. I'm just going to throw it out.	The execution might not have been ideal, but this is a great concept. Keep trying!
Sorry, this is just a draft. I know it isn't any good.	There are many things about this draft that work. Let's look at what we can adjust.
My vocabulary is all wrong. I don't know enough big words.	Big words can interfere with your voice. Keeping it simple is actually better.
Nobody will like this. I don't want to show it to anyone.	Let's think about why you are worried about this and look at what is good first.

By the time students reach their secondary years in education, too many have lost their faith in their own worth as writers. Unfortunately, as the thoughts in the left-hand column of Table 1.2 indicate, a harsh lens of judgment can cloud creativity or voice and prioritize some aspects of written work (often mechanics or structure) over others. When teachers coach students to find what works about a piece of writing before tearing it to pieces, the benefits are significant.

English professor Betty Flowers (1981) identifies the four voices that exist within all of us when we write: Madman, Architect, Carpenter, and Judge. These roles speak to the process of creating, structuring, refining, and critiquing our work. With all writers, the voice of the Judge can be so strong that it completely halts progress. When teachers see students who are stuck on one phrase or paragraph and are unable to move forward, it often occurs because they are reading back over what they have done, rewriting endlessly to produce something that might be better. On the opposite end of the spectrum, students who unleash a steady stream of sentences without paying attention to organized thought have leaned into the Madman, whose ingenuity overpowers structure.

To interrupt the myth of the "bad" writer, teachers must strive to help students find balance in their approach to writing. Without it, students are apt to focus on any deficiencies in one of the four writing voices that Flowers defines and conclude that their writing is holistically poor in quality. To create clarity and validity around the pieces of the writing process that come together to make a final product, the first step teachers must take is to introduce students to a writing process that they may not have encountered before in their academic courses. In other words, it is imperative to let go of our current obsession with structure over content, voice, and depth.

Listening to All Voices:
The Power of Creative Nonfiction

The link between the application of an accessible lens to writing instruction and solid teaching practice that welcomes a variety of ways to present ideas in writing cannot be underestimated. Consider the limitations that are inherent in how we teach students to write. If we want to elicit automatic groans from students, all we need to do is utter this phrase "five paragraph essay." Their reaction will be as strong as it is immediate. Strangely, while very few students will ever say that they enjoy working within such a rigid framework, they have a difficult time moving past it to compose more creatively designed pieces once they become comfortable with the classic setup of introduction, three body paragraphs, and con-clusion. As a result, nearly every essay a teacher reads sounds the same, with the necessary structural components ticked off a checklist while important elements like voice and creativity take a backseat—if they're in the car at all. Writing instruction in the secondary grades is hyper-focused on organization, but to move past the myth of the "bad" writer, a divergent instructional approach is necessary.

To get students out of the writing rut we create for them, teachers can begin by broadening the limited definition of "essay" that preteens and teens have lived with for too long. Depending on who we might ask, there are at least eight different types of essays in existence, and very likely more than that. They range from expository to process-driven, and most do not appear in secondary writing instruction. Students may read an essay that primarily defines something, particularly in a science course, but they are not often asked to engage in this style of writing themselves. By not only sharing the various types of compositions that exist but also providing the opportunity to experiment with letting students create their own versions, teachers open up a narrowly defined term and remove some of the stigma associated with the dreaded term "essay."

Once students begin to understand that writing in the nonfiction realm may be more open than they realized, the next step is to tap into the power of creative nonfiction. Toward the latter part of each school year, I used to assign a project that was inspired by a humorous piece on how *not* to write entitled "How to Say Nothing in 500 Words" by Paul McHenry Roberts (1958). After the class read McRoberts's advice together and applied his words to their own writing mishaps, I would give students a challenge that they were ready for, now that the year was coming to a close. The assignment was simply this: Write 500 words about any topic at all, provided that the essay is true. The type of essay itself was up for grabs. Students could write a narrative (the most popular choice), or they could try their hand at descriptive or expository writing. However, the goal remained to write in any form, about anything real, with focus and a strong voice.

Not unpredictably, this assignment scared as many students as it inspired. Never having been faced with so much academic freedom, they were unsure of what to do. "What should I write about?" they asked, coming to me for help. Invariably, I would respond, "What are you interested in?" Sometimes, that helped. More often, I needed to give them someplace to start, like making a list of all the things they found annoying or exciting, to get the brainstorming process fully underway. As my classes grappled with having fewer writing limits than they remembered having since perhaps their elementary years, it became clear that when students tell teachers they want more creativity, they probably mean it; however, after years of being drilled on formats around topic sentences, examples, and commentary, they need to be retaught how to let their inner Madman out.

When it came time to share the 500 words about anything at all, I conducted an experiment to see whether students had been able to prioritize the goal of letting their writing voices be heard. Instead of asking students to share out loud, they printed out copies of their essays with no names on top, but a number instead. We scattered the essays around the classroom and students did a "gallery walk" around the room to read one another's work. As they rotated, they carried a notebook with them to make notations about whose name might match up with the number on top of the page. Having been in the classroom together for many months, they were trying to guess at the identity of the writer based on both the content of the essay and the voice of the writer. To be sure, some essays were easier to guess at than others; I had a student who was a passionate and vocal fan of Billie Holliday, and her essay on the topic was clearly nobody else's work. However, other students were harder to figure out. I walked around with my class, knowing more than they did (I had seen many drafts), but also engaged in watching them try and figure out whose work was whose.

In the end, most of the essays were matched with the correct writers, but a handful (anywhere between five and ten) remained elusive until the class engaged in the Big Reveal. Those who had eluded their peers were often pleased with themselves, mainly because they managed to maintain an aura of mystery around who they were. Some of them were surprised, having left "Easter egg"-type clues in their essays for people to find that went unnoticed. And always, there was the delight of students in one another as they expressed wonder and amusement at what their peers had created: "That was *you*? That was so awesome!"

Opening the writing experience to place more emphasis on the value of ideas and the collective power of peer feedback helps teachers achieve an approach that builds student identity productively both in and out of the classroom. However, that is only the beginning of facilitating an inclusive space that welcomes all voices. When students have more positive instructional experiences, it would be nice to say that they will no longer feel the need to use The Disclaimer. Unfortunately, the process of deconstructing years of explicit or implicit bias around writing ability does not end overnight. However, with persistence and awareness, skillful teachers can slowly chip away at the faulty assumptions that students have held to be true for far too long, paving the way for new perspectives.

Cross-Content Strategy

The value of learning from teachers who have experience in an entirely different subject area is immeasurable. Throughout this book, a variety of cross-content activities and strategies will be presented to establish, affirm, and validate student academic identity. While many of these tools have centered on the writing process, which appears across all content areas, there are any number of ways to dig more deeply into the core of student belonging that do not involve explicitly engaging in writing instruction.

The power of teachers to help one another is formidable, and that philosophy guides the sharing of cross-content strategies. Rather than share only resources that I have used in my own instructional experience, I turned to seasoned teaching colleagues in a range of content areas and locations to share what they do in their classrooms to prioritize student academic identity. These strategies, which are located at the close of several chapters and have been successfully implemented with a diverse population of students, are shared here for immediate and practical use. It might be natural to first consult the strategies closest to one's own content area, but I strongly recommend reading them all. Our learning targets overlap more than we might think, and these skillful teachers exemplify this interconnectedness with their thoughtful ideas for instruction.

Physics, High School
Contributor: James Schafer

Activity:
For every unit in introductory physics, students are expected to create their own physics problem. After having seen examples modeled in class, through homework, and in their texts, students have the opportunity to craft their own version of a problem for classmates to solve.

Goal:
The purposes of this assignment are:

- Give students the opportunity to demonstrate proficiency with vocabulary in a particular physics unit.
- Help students meet learning targets in the application of formulas.
- Support students to achieve the standard in algebraic manipulation and solving of equations related to a particular physics unit.
- Promote peer-to-peer interactions in the solving, editing, and discussing of the problem.
- Allow students to showcase their creativity.
- Empower students to feel ownership of the content.

Method:
1. On the top half of a document, students construct a problem that is similar in difficulty and style to what they have done in class, including diagrams as appropriate.
2. They are then asked to create the solution (showing all steps and work) on the bottom half of the sheet on which they typed the problem. Typically, students will hand write the solution, though some may elect to type the solution.
3. Students bring their problem with its solution to class, and

then class time is dedicated to students trading and solving one another's problems.

4. After having worked on another student's problem, there is time to discuss any issues with clarity, vocabulary use, or other issues with the problem itself. There is also a focus on discussing the solution: Was sufficient work shown? Were the correct values substituted in for the correct variables? Was the mathematical solving done correctly? Were correct units shown? And so forth.

5. Following multiple peer reviews, students are given an opportunity to revise their problem prior to final submission.

Motivation:

This writing opportunity allows students to not only demonstrate their level of comprehension with the content, but to also make problems more relevant to their experience and to demonstrate their creativity. With peer reviews prior to final grading, students are given time to clarify and refine their work. Through their use of language, the teacher can assess whether students are using terms and ideas appropriately. This method also gets students away from what is often a rote method of just attempted pattern matching when trying to solve physics problems. With this assignment, there are multiple areas in which all students can showcase their level of understanding.

For an additional level of motivation, the teacher can offer to use the best problems (in a modified format) as questions on future assessments, which hopefully excites students to do their best work. Additionally, knowing that a peer's problem may be used, students are encouraged to solve more problems from peers outside of class if they feel that they need additional practice.

Results:

STUDENT SAMPLE #1: STUDENT-CREATED PROBLEM AND SOLUTION

Mr. Shafer loves doing trampoline tricks, and enjoys showing them off to Tonka. Mr. Schafer starts on a trampoline raised 2 m above the ground and jumps off of it with a velocity of 5 m/s and angle of 30 above the horizontal. How far will Mr. Schafer land from where he started?

	x	y
Vo	$2.5\sqrt{3}$	2.5
Vf		
a	0 m/s^2	-9.8 m/s^2
d	find!	-2 m
t	0.943	0.943

5

2.5

30

$2.5\sqrt{3}$

$$d = Vot + \tfrac{1}{2}at^2$$
$$-2 = 2.5t - 4.9t^2$$
$$4.9t^2 - 2.5t - 2 = 0$$
$$t = 0.943$$

$$d = Vot + \tfrac{1}{2}at^2$$
$$d = 2.5\sqrt{3} \times 0.943 =$$
$$d = 4.08$$

Answer: Mr. Schafer landed 4.08 m
away from where he started.

STUDENT SAMPLE #2: NARRATIVE PROBLEM BY KATE PATRABANSH

In a distant galaxy somewhere, far across the universe, there is a planet called Clymedes. It is hidden, tucked away, but its people are not so different from those of Earth. One thing that is important to note about Clymedes is that there is no such thing as gravity, and there is instead a force called jerkin that pulls things to the right. Because of this, there are constantly objects hurtling through the air at terminal velocity. Like these objects, the people of Clymedes are affected by jerkin, but they can use sheer willpower to remain stationary and are able to go about their daily lives as humans would. (All the buildings are latched firmly to the ground.)

One morning, a young girl was crouched on top of the roof of a building and looking up at the sky, which was just brightening with the colors of dawn. She seemed to be waiting for something. All of a sudden, an object loomed toward her from her left, but she ducked it nimbly, as all Clymedans learn to do at a young age. A few seconds later, a pencil came hurtling toward her, and she closed her hand around it soundlessly moments before it touched her throat. Coming to life suddenly, she stood. One hand held the pencil while the other tied a tracker around it. It was time to test her theory: that jerkin would not affect motion in the vertical direction. She bounced twice on the balls of her foot before releasing the pencil skyward at 23 m/s and at an angle 86° to the right. It arced up for a perfect moment before, inevitably, its path bent rightward. But the girl smiled, joy and wonder evident on her face, for the pencil was still moving upward. She had not been wrong after all.

Acceleration due to jerkin on Clymedes is 1.7 m/s 2, regardless of the mass of the object. At what time should the girl check her tracker monitor if she wants to see the horizontal displacement meet and surpass the vertical displacement? How high will the pencil be at this point (in km)? (The building is 65.617 ft tall.)

CHAPTER 2

The Complexity of Class Participation

Speaking Up

Hallie walks into her ninth-grade English class, sitting down with a familiar sense of dread. Many of the students around her are animated, chatting with one another in the last few precious moments before the bell rings. For Hallie, that excitement is irritating. Thanks to the brilliance of computer scheduling, there is not one person in this class she can call a friend. Nobody bothers her, but over the past couple of months since school began, nobody has tried to get to know her, either.

The teacher walks in, and Hallie suppresses an outer eye roll. Mr. Brock may be popular, but he acts like she is invisible. For reasons she can't quite explain to anyone, Hallie is uncomfortable around Mr. Brock. His extreme friendliness doesn't extend to her, and while he is pleasant, a clear message emanates from him on the rare instances they interact: *Who are you, again?*

Mr. Brock fiddles with his computer to get it going. "Take out your books, people," he says. "We'll get going in just a minute."

Hallie digs into her bag and pulls out *To Kill a Mockingbird*. Classmates around her grumble about the book, but she actually doesn't mind this one. The courtroom scenes are suspenseful, and it's not that hard to read.

It sure beats Shakespeare, and she knows that *Romeo and Juliet* is coming down the pike later in the semester.

At the front of the room, Mr. Brock has gotten his technology in order, and the agenda for the day is posted on the smartboard. "Here's the plan," he announces. "Instead of discussing the chapters we read for homework, I'd like to do something different." He points at the board, and Hallie reads the directions in front of her:

> Pick a central character from the chapters we read for home-
> work. Write a one-page diary entry from the perspective of that
> character, inserting any details from the book as relevant.

"I'd like everyone to write for 10 minutes and be prepared to share when we're done," Mr. Brock says. "Feel free to be creative. Have fun with writing in a different voice."

While Hallie dislikes class discussions and never feels confident enough to speak up, she loves to write. It gives her a chance to process her ideas, and in this case, she can even pretend to be someone else. Deciding that Scout gets enough first-person airtime, Hallie decides to write from the perspective of her least favorite character: Mayella Ewell.

Over the next ten minutes, Hallie is happier than usual. Her pen flies across the page and she forgets about everyone and everything around her. As she embodies the perspective of Mayella, Hallie tries to connect more with the character's feelings of helplessness in the face of a domineering father and less with Mayella's racist ideals. The latter makes her too uncomfortable to write about, whereas Hallie can identify with the experience of having adults she does not admire tell her what to do.

She is so absorbed in her work that when Mr. Brock breaks in with a two-minute warning, she barely registers his voice. Finally, she hears the alarm bell go off to signify the end of the writing period and she looks up. All around her, kids are surveying their work, though a few are still adding final words. Hallie looks down at her own notebook and is startled to realize that she has gone far past the one-page limit. Her composition notebook entry is three and a half pages long.

"Time to share," Mr. Brock says, and Hallie instantly feels both nervous and excited. Deep down, she wants to read her diary entry aloud, but she is afraid of what the class will think. Maybe Mr. Brock will do random calling and she will have a chance to be picked. Instead, her spirits fall when he asks, "Who wants to go first?"

At the beginning of the year, Hallie raised her hand and volunteered to speak a few times. With one exception, Mr. Brock never called on her until many others had already spoken, and by then, her thoughts were no longer relevant to the conversation. The one time he did call on her first, another student interrupted her, shared the same idea first, and wasn't even chastised. Since then, Hallie has thought it best to keep her thoughts to herself.

Now, as hands shoot into the air, Hallie does not move a muscle. One by one, her classmates are called on. Many of them have chosen to write from Scout's perspective, and Hallie sighs internally. *Harper Lee already wrote that*, she thinks, *and she did it better*. One student shares an entry from Jem's point of view, and another writes as Atticus. But nobody has bothered to take on the Ewells at all, and Hallie finds herself wondering if she took too great a risk in writing from an antagonist's perspective.

When it comes time to move on, Mr. Brock begins to collect the journals. "Those were great," he says. "I'm sure I'll read a lot more fantastic responses that we didn't have a chance to get to."

Hallie's shrug is just barely visible. She knows he probably won't read her journal, or even if he does, he won't do anything but skim it and put a check mark on her work. As the class settles down to work on the next agenda item, Hallie looks at the clock on the wall. There are 23 more minutes left in the period, and then it's finally lunchtime. At least that is something she can look forward to.

The Quiet Kid: Transcending the Stereotype

Children learn from an early age that being assertive relays significant advantages. If Mr. Brock from the prior scenario stops and thinks about Hallie, he likely attaches a label to her, whether he realizes it or not: she is The Quiet Kid. Having encountered many similar children in the course of his career, he doesn't have strong opinions about learners that he assumes are socially introverted. These students do not say much, but their grades are generally at least mediocre, if not a little better. They cause no discipline problems, and they seem nice enough. There's not much else to be said, is there?

But as anyone who has been The Quiet Kid (or who has parented or been close friends with The Quiet Kid) knows, there really is no such person. Silence is one sign of discomfort, rising out of situations in which people lack a sense of belonging. Children who are highly vocal at home and with friends may clam up in a classroom if the teacher is oblivious to their presence, if fellow classmates are unfamiliar or intimidating, or if nobody seems to value what they have to say. Beyond the social damage that being dismissed can confer, there are also academic consequences to being The Quiet Kid.

Students who are stigmatized as being "quiet" also do not receive the same advantages as their more vocal peers because their needs are easily overlooked when more assertive students are clamoring for attention. Essentially a form of implicit bias, when more reticent students are ignored by adults (inadvertently or not), it leads to lower levels of access to any number of opportunities and limits growth on common performance measures like grades and assessments. It also permanently alters students' sense of identity, often to their detriment. This widespread issue can only be addressed if teachers recognize the inherent value of all students they work with, not just those who express themselves in ways that are more externally visible.

The key to building the visibility of learners who tend to go unnoticed lies in how we frame relationships with students. Many teachers have a reputation for being popular or well-liked, but does that mean they form genuine connections with *all* their students, even the quieter ones? Building teacher-to-student relationships is often misunderstood as a personal endeavor. While there is value to knowing what movies students enjoy or opening a classroom at lunchtime to create opportunities for socializing, these efforts do nothing to build the kind of safe academic space that quieter students need to trust teachers with their ideas.

To send the overt message that all contributions to discourse are valid, reframing how student participation functions is key. The classic setup of asking a question and waiting for one desired answer is designed to silence internal processors who are not comfortable with taking the chance that their answers will be dismissed. Similarly, any time we expect students to produce or parrot back a specific response that aligns with our own line of thinking, that closes off more hesitant voices in the classroom who realize that more divergent ideas are not welcome. That is why vocal students are not necessarily the most critical thinkers, whereas quieter students might be holding back on sharing contributions which hold immense value to the learning that takes place in a classroom.

To combat the very natural tendency to call on students who seem the most eager to speak or who validate the teacher's own thought process, actively incorporating inclusive strategies that increase the participation of each learner in the room empowers all students to feel a sense of validation. Box 2.1 shares a helpful bank of strategies that teachers can use to draw out even the most reticent of learners, as well as the rationale behind each activity and the benefits it confers to students.

BOX 2.1

Strategy #1: Circle Discussion

Students sit in a circle to discuss an accessible and engaging concept the teacher has presented, new or familiar. Each student has two index cards which represent a comment. During the discussion, each time students share a thought, they throw an index card into the middle of the room. When they run out of index cards, they must sit quietly and listen to the conversation. All students are expected to use at least one of their cards.

WHY?

With a circle discussion, the design allows students to both step back and listen more, and also to sit up and speak more. While the discussion occurs, teachers take a backseat and note the ideas that students share without breaking into the conversation, both for the purpose of becoming more familiar with the interpersonal dynamics of their classes and for determining what students know about the topic.

Strategy #2: Silent Discourse

The teacher poses an open-ended, complex question or topic to guide class discussion. Rather than engage in vocal discourse, students write their names at the top of a piece of paper and share an opening thought.

Then, they pass their papers in a predetermined direction and respond to one another in writing. When one series of ideas is exhausted on the page, they are permitted to start a new train of discussion.

WHY?

When all students in the class make contributions at the same time and share them with one another, the equitable distribution of participation becomes a reality. Every individual has a voice, and students are able to focus on ideas, not people. As an added benefit, the teacher can collect the papers at the end and read the discussion threads to see how students are receiving the content, and to use what everyone shared as guidance for a subsequent lesson.

Strategy #3: Share Rotation

Rather than asking for student volunteers to share their work aloud, rotate a variety of ways for them to showcase their work. Options include:

- *Gallery walk*. Students move through the classroom and read one another's work, leaving encouraging notes to one another or productive feedback as they go.

- *Small group share*. Students pass their papers around (or read aloud quietly) in a group that is composed of no more than four people. All members are expected to share. Then, a predesignated member of each small group (this changes each time) both paraphrases what each group member wrote, and then explains one thing that was admirable about each project. Or, time permitting, all group members could take turns paraphrasing and praising one another.

- *Quick view*. Rather than ask students to share a whole product, ask them to pick a favorite paragraph (or perhaps even just a few sentences) to share with the class. Then, collect the papers and randomly pull them out of the pile to ask students to share. Note that while students are pre-alerted to being called upon and should be ready, an adjustment that can be made earlier in the year is to invite any apprehensive students to mark the tops of their papers with an "X" or similar if they do not wish to read aloud.

WHY?

While equitable or random calling practices have been touted in recent years as a way to even out the voices that everyone hears each class period, they can be difficult to implement multiple times in a class period. In addition, when students write or develop longer-term products, random calling is sometimes not as useful as one of the strategies outlined above. By using any of the provided rotation processes, teachers can plan in advance for how students will make contributions while students will appreciate the variety of opportunities that are given to display their efforts.

Strategy #4: Post-Its

With this small but mighty classroom supply staple, students can write brief thoughts on any topic (anonymously or otherwise) on sticky notes and post their ideas on the wall. Then, classmates have the opportunity to put check marks next to the Post-Its that resonate for any reason at all, or the teacher can gather a few to highlight a specific point about what the class is learning.

WHY?

In addition to the obvious benefit of opening up more safe avenues for student participation that this strategy provides, both students and teachers can use this activity as a test of temperature or to engage in critical thinking about what others know, which concepts are thought-provoking, and what learning might need to take place next.

The thought that goes into ensuring that each voice is heard in some form or other must be paramount in a teacher's mind when designing strategies for participation that are more inclusive of voices that are not heard as frequently. Furthermore, discussion does not need to be vocal. Depending on the learning goal, students are able to contribute their ideas in a variety of modalities using the tools in Box 2.1.

In a moving piece about his own experiences as The Quiet Kid, teacher and writer John Spencer (2022) describes the struggle he encountered when called upon to speak:

> *If I wasn't prepared when a teacher called on me, I'd freeze up.*
> *I'd shake and sweat, stammering and sputtering over my words.*
> *A few kids would mock me, but most students would stare in*
> *shock as I struggled. In most cases, the teachers would assume*
> *I hadn't been paying attention, when the truth was I needed to*
> *work through my responses alone before sharing my thoughts*
> *with the class.*

Spencer also explains that he developed coping strategies for avoiding this kind of experience, like trying to proactively stay one step ahead of the teacher and jot down his responses to questions in advance. However, the attention and energy involved with this kind of maneuvering could not always be sustained, and he invariably fell prey to all the wrong assumptions described above.

It is the teacher's responsibility to make sure that students do not have traumatic experiences when they learn in our classrooms. Part of our willingness to reach quieter learners involves the agility to recognize that no matter what we do, some students will not feel comfortable speaking out in class. That is not anything to take personally, or to try to force into submission. Instead, figuring out how students can contribute their voices in a variety of ways increases their likelihood of growing confident enough to one day be more vocal. That is why the strategies featured in Table 2.1 are so important: They provide that entry point for students who do not like to speak and give them a way to be part of the class without making their hesitance noticeable.

There is a difference between being an introvert and being perceived as quiet for not speaking. Many introverts are perfectly comfortable sharing their viewpoints as vocally as the next person. They may not enjoy crowds, or it might be preferable for an introvert to focus on making meaning of ideas internally rather than externally processing them. Being labeled "quiet," however, is an entirely different representation, and one that tends to be inaccurate. All we need to do is follow so-called "quiet" kids home and we see exactly how voluble (hint: very) they get within a zone of safety. Therefore, teachers must create an environment that makes everyone feel secure enough to make contributions. When that happens, students who have not been accustomed to speaking up grow more comfortable with how their ideas are received, and a trusting relationship with their teacher grows right along with their confidence, ultimately resulting in heightened achievement.

Building profound relationships among students and teachers is not just about rapport—it is about creating the kind of trust that leads to academic success and achievement for all students, loud or quiet. When student voices are marginalized, the consequence (intended or not) is a decrease in performance. Thankfully, teachers can create a more inclusive space that serves a greater range of learners by increasing their repertoire of instructional strategies to provide students who are reluctant to speak with alternate ways to demonstrate engagement in class. Applying these changes to classroom practice right away will result in endless rewards for students who have been denied a way to share their voices for too long.

Vocal Learner or Active Learner?

In every fresh school year, I used to encounter the same piece of informal data about two weeks in. Until I learned to be a little more analytical, this piece of data was something I noticed, but not something I did anything about. Later, though, I would come to see the significance of what seemed minor on the surface, but went so much deeper.

Here is what it looked like: Picture an engaging, highly vocal learner. This student chooses to sit toward the front of the classroom if given the option, walks in with a smile, builds rapport effortlessly with teachers and peers alike, and quickly becomes a go-to person for the teacher when uncomfortable silence threatens to take over a discussion. This individual is easy to talk to, loves to be relied on, and generally makes the classroom a happier place to be.

Strangely enough, when grades start to come in, there is a seeming disconnect. Though this vocal, dynamic student has shown keen intelligence and demonstrated welcome insight in class conversation, there is a lack of consistency in performance to support this behavior. Assignment or assessment grades for this student might not be abysmal, but they are often lower than expected. Concepts that seemed to be clearly understood in a verbal exchange are muddled or even wrong in writing, and there is no evidence that the student is as competent as assumed.

The first several years of teaching, I explained this unusual dissonance that I saw in some students by attributing it to the increasingly controversial theory of multiple intelligences, which can result in labeling students inaccurately or unfairly. To bear out that idea, I assumed that students who were strong in one communication method might struggle in another and left it at that. It never occurred to me to seek further information until, several years down the road with more experience, I began to wonder about what it means to be an active learner.

Active learning is a term that is widely used, and it is also broadly defined. According to Dr. Cynthia Brame (2016), associate director of the Center for Teaching at Vanderbilt University: "Approaches that promote active learning focus more on developing students' skills than on transmitting information and require that students do something—read, discuss, write—that requires higher-order thinking" (p. 1). The part of this definition that matters is the reference to "higher-order thinking" that makes ubiquitous processes like reading, writing, and discussion more meaningful. When Bloom's taxonomy was developed, it helped teachers everywhere delineate the distinction between students passively doing something and their active engagement in a critical thinking process.

To illustrate this concept further, think again about the vocal student at the front of the room whose academic performance does not seem to match contributions to class discussions. Does verbal output represent the sort of comprehension that allows students to make connections among a variety of ideas, or is something else going on? Perhaps vocal students, who may also be socially adept and therefore accustomed to picking up on various cues their teachers emit, have an entirely different approach that teachers overlook. Rather than representing an elevated understanding of content matter, their participation might be a skillful smokescreen that appears to be learning acquisition, but is really a way for teachers to continue transmitting the ideas in their brains to be parroted back without the need to consider other points of view.

In certain situations, vocal students are surprisingly passive from a cognitive point of view. They may appear to be active learners, but it is easy to confuse a strong personality coupled with frequent participation for achievement of learning outcomes. No wonder, then, it comes as a shock when their work is turned in and does not match the behavior exhibited in class.

Does this mean that vocal students always display this academic dissonance? Absolutely not. Many vocal learners are active learners, but some are not. And conversely, some of the quietest learners in the classroom (think back to Hallie) are the most active. Unfortunately, teachers who do not find ways for all students to show their learning within the class period wind up believing that the more silent learners are also the most passive, which is a huge misconception that acts as a disservice to students.

At its core, active learning relies on a collaborative, student-centered approach. As Brame (2016) explains, "active learning approaches also often embrace the use of cooperative learning groups, a constructivist-based practice that places particular emphasis on the contribution that social interaction can make" (p. 2). One would think that students embrace such a model, but an unexpected complication of creating a learning environment around active methods is sometimes a show of student resistance. After years of a more passive experience, many students can be loath to do something different, even if the end result will be more fulfilling. In "Students Think Lectures Are Best, But Research Suggests They're Wrong," *Edutopia* editor Youki Terada (2019) cites a study published in the *Proceedings of the National Academy of Sciences* (PNAS). As Terada shares, the research study showed that "strategies that require low cognitive effort—such as passively listening to a lecture—are often perceived by students to be more effective than active strategies such as hands-on experimentation and group problem-solving." Why might that be?

PNAS researchers Louis Deslauriers et al. (2019) answer this question when they "identify an inherent student bias against active learning that can limit its effectiveness and may hinder the wide adoption of these methods." Essentially, students perceive that they are most successful in traditional, teacher-directed classrooms. There are any number of reasons they might feel this way, from having never experienced anything different to worrying about what might happen if they are asked to do what feels like more. To combat this problem, the study suggests that teachers explicitly share with students why a more active approach is better and then continue to reinforce its benefits: "The success of active learning will be greatly enhanced if students accept that it leads to deeper learning and acknowledge that it may sometimes feel like exactly the opposite is true" (Deslauriers et al., 2019).

Teaching students is not just about communicating content; it is also about being instructive about how to access learning. If we are not explicit about the "why" behind the ways in which class is structured, students will form their own assumptions about what works. It is not enough, therefore, to create a student-centered classroom model and expect everyone to get on board without knowing the rationale behind an active learning approach. Instead, developing a space in which all learners (vocal or otherwise) can flourish is also dependent upon explaining what is happening as it occurs, gathering student voice along the way, and course-correcting as needed.

To get started on the active learning journey, Table 2.1 shares two columns: a list of strategies, and the benefits of each one to share with students. That way, each time we try one of the tools in practice, students will understand how this approach supports their growth with a clear explanation of the "why" behind each activity.

TABLE 2.1

Active Learning Strategy	Benefits and Results
The Big Question Midway through sharing new information, the teacher pauses and asks students to write down an area of confusion so far. Then, students either post their questions on the wall and respond in writing or hand them to the teacher to share with the group anonymously.	• Clears up confusion • Encourages a culture of welcoming mistakes and misconceptions • Normalizes not knowing and asking questions • Allows students to communicate in a variety of modalities • Gives everyone a voice
Connection, Prediction Before starting a daily objective, students pose a question or idea that makes a connection to prior learning. Then, they develop a prediction about what they are about to learn and share their thoughts with classmates via pairings or small groups.	• Encourages the use of higher-order, critical thinking skills • Provides an avenue for students to share at low risk (i.e., in smaller groups) rather than in front of the class • Allows the teacher to see how students make meaning of the daily objective in front of them

Question Everything For a specific timeframe within the class period, students are asked to phrase any response to a question in a shared space (an online document, chart paper, board, etc.) as an open-ended question. Then, students answer the question by posing yet another question of their own in the same space.	• Engages students in critical questioning • All participants have a chance to respond to one another in an accessible space • The teacher can be on the look-out for misconceptions and adjust instruction accordingly
Images and Inspiration Using a visual image (a photograph, drawing or similar, the teacher asks students to "free write" for a short period of time about what the image inspires. Depending on the course subject, students could write their conjectures about what they see or engage in a more creative approach.	• Allows students to make their own meaning of an image before the teacher directs learning more specifically toward the daily lesson • Encourages students to learn in a different way (i.e., visually) • Helps to facilitate a more inductive approach to course content
One Sentence For an upcoming extended writing project that may be intimidating, ask students to write just one sentence from the assigned prompt. Then, put them in small groups to examine one another's sentences and discuss the challenges they face.	• Embraces the concept that all learners struggle, and that collaboration is key to surmounting obstacles • Teaches students with multiple points of view to help one another • Breaks a formidable task into more manageable chunks
Rephrase, Please! Sometimes, ideas get lost in translation. In this activity, students are asked to take the key ideas taught during direct instruction and phrase them in their own words. They can then post their phrases on a wall, share in groups, or be called upon randomly.	• Helps students make meaning of new concepts in their own heads • Acts as a check for understanding for the teacher to see where struggles might still exist • Empowers students to think critically about the salient ideas presented
Stump the Teacher Students form groups and create a series of quiz questions on course content. Then, groups take turns posing questions in an attempt to stump the teacher. If the teacher cannot answer enough questions correctly, the class wins!	• This gamification technique increases student engagement • Teachers provide students with the opportunity to engage in a role reversal • By creating the quizzes, students learn material more actively

Active learning is dependent upon the act of critical thinking. With the strategies and accompanying rationale provided within Table 2.1, teachers working with multiple grade levels in a variety of content areas can find at least a few approaches that work to increase the involvement of everyone in the room.

Tempting though it might be to rely on vocal students to carry student discourse each day past the point of awkwardness and toward whatever a teacher might wish to highlight, resisting that urge is key to ensuring that every child in the room is an active learner. Even the loudest students in the room who verbally process information may be more passive than we suppose. So, finding more effective ways to involve all students in each day's learning is an effort that is well worth the time. That way, when a teacher leaves the classroom thinking, "Wow. They were really with me today," that thought will apply to not just the few students who always like to talk—it will also accurately represent the experience of the entire class.

Separating Grading from Participation: A Better Path

On the first day of school, students file into an assembly that will share what are known as the "Ps and Ps"—policies and procedures—for the upcoming year. At the front of the room, the principal stands with a microphone, welcoming everyone. Once students settle down, she begins a slideshow. "And I want to remind everyone," the principal says, "that if you have more than six unexcused absences in a class, the teacher can lower your overall semester percentage by one point, with another point for each subsequent absence."

In the audience, some students look apprehensive, while others roll their eyes. One sixth-grader, new to middle school, turns to the older girl next to her. "But what if I'm doing really well in the class?"

The girl, by now a jaded seventh-grader, shakes her head. "Don't worry. This is only for unexcused absences, like the kind for skipping class. If your grades are good, you're probably not doing that."

The new student nods and says no more, but deep down, she is worried. She gets every cold that comes around, and her mom works nights and often misses the chance to call the school and excuse her. What if she winds up losing points for being sick? She really cares about school, and she loves to learn, but this seems unfair. As she listens to the rest of the "Ps and Ps," the sixth-grader wonders just how hard middle school is going to be.

Traditionally, American schools grade students in two areas: learning and behavior. Students understand the former a little better because it is more logical. For example, if a child is asked to write three sentences and only writes one, a lower grade is a consequence that makes sense because the learning criterion is unmet. For behavior-based grading, which assigns a quantifiable measure to anything from attendance to perceived engagement, the waters become significantly muddier. Adults make too many assumptions about what kids understand, when in reality, a lot gets lost in translation. Think about the term "participation grade." This phrase is all too common in schools, with the idea that by adding the qualifier of "participation," students will understand that being assessed for how much they contribute is somehow not connected to their academic performance in course content. But why, some students may wonder, does their overall grade drop when the participation grade is low? If they understand what they learn, why are they being penalized for how much they say?

When we consider the ways in which teachers build trust with students, having a grading system that is built upon what students consider fair matters. If we assign negative consequences to participation, two things happen: not only do students associate being engaged in the class with a penalty, but they are also more likely to think that all their grades are tinged with bias. Behavior-based grades are personal, which denies the very foundation of what a grade is meant to do: objectively measure student performance in relation to a content standard. The result is a learning space in which students do not feel comfortable taking academic risks.

In classrooms where writing makes up a significant portion of instructional time, students who feel uncertain about how their contributions are received are not going to be as willing to share their work, both with their teachers and with one another. If the teacher's goal is to increase student confidence in sharing ideas, starting with building awareness around participation is a first step in helping students understand how involved they appear to be in the learning from the point of view of an external observer. Tables 2.2 and 2.3 offer a simple chart (one blank and one filled out as an example) that guides students through a process of thinking about what they contribute to a class, where they might be holding back and why, and how to hold themselves responsible for growing their learning presence.

TABLE 2.2

Participation Self-Assessment		
How much do I talk?	Should I be doing more?	What might help me grow?

TABLE 2.3

Participation Self-Assessment		
How much do I talk?	Should I be doing more?	What might help me grow?
Maybe I talk about once or twice a week? I don't say much in this class. It's not my favorite subject, and I don't have that many friends here.	My grade is OK, but it could be better. Nobody seems to think much about what I say, so I keep thoughts to myself.	If I talked more, it might help me understand the work. I will try to participate more.

For students who are too often ignored, a chart like the one in Tables 2.2 and 2.3 will aid in their understanding of how they engage in a class beyond their inner selves. In the example provided in Table 2.3, the student realizes that not participating in class might be interfering with achieving learning goals. This kind of reflective opportunity to consider how we process information is far more valuable to increasing student progress than providing an arbitrary grade for participation. Other strategies for increasing participation, like the ones highlighted in Table 2.1, also go a long way toward bringing forth student voice.

Naysayers will argue that a solid rationale for behavior-based grading falls in line with teaching students how to navigate complex challenges. Best-selling writer and teacher Jessica Lahey (2013) argues in *The Atlantic* that "A student who is unwilling to stand up for herself and tell me that she does not understand the difference between an adverb and a verb is also less likely to stand up for herself if she is being harassed or pressured in other areas of her life." While that point is well taken, teaching students to speak up and grading them for doing so are two entirely different propositions. Grades are an external motivator, and one to which only certain children respond. If a student is hesitant to speak and the result is a lower grade, the consequence may be a lowering of involvement in the class, not an increase. When faced with what they perceive as failure, many children give up, especially if their struggles are internal. If adults do not notice this decline in confidence, they cannot realize there is a problem to fix. Furthermore, the conditional nature of participation grades makes it hard to break out of a cycle in which students believe they have to change who they are to be successful.

On the other hand, if reticent students are gradually made to feel not just safe as learners but effective as well, their own belief in their academic validity will gradually lead to an increase in participation. First, that may look like a series of smaller contributions, but as time goes on, they will gather their sense of self-efficacy and emerge from their proverbial shells, ready to be more visibly engaged each day.

Safe Zones

"It's Game Day!"

Kids walk into Ms. Diaz's composition class, excited for the promised writing game. The schedule is shorter today thanks to the end of the marking period, and everyone is worn out from getting so much work turned in as things wind down. It will be nice to kick back for once and just have a good time.

"Okay," Ms. Diaz announces, clapping her hands together. "We have an abbreviated period, so let's move quickly. Circle formation, everyone, and bring your notebooks with you."

The class has rehearsed this before, and in less than two minutes, all students have moved their chairs into a neat circle, notebooks and pens at the ready.

"Today's game is . . . alphabet round robin," Ms. Diaz says.

There are some laughs, some groans, and one kid says, "Uh oh."

Taking it all in stride, Ms. Diaz reminds them of the rules. "So, just a few details. You have to start each sentence with the next letter of the alphabet of the sentence that came before. Everything needs to stay school appropriate. And please, try to have it make sense. Read what came before it. The challenge is to write a coherent story, not to sabotage one another." At this last point, she raises an eyebrow and there is more laughter.

One student calls out, "You forgot the Vegas rule!"

"I did," Ms. Diaz says, smiling. "Safe space, everyone. It all stays here. You ready? We're passing clockwise. I'm so excited." She picks up her own notebook and pen. "Let's do it!"

Immediately, everyone focuses on their notebooks, the room quiet except for the sound of pens scratching on paper. As students finish each sentence, they pass notebooks in one direction and receive another, building upon one another's stories. Every now and then, the silence is punctuated with giggling, the occasional "you've gotta be kidding me," or someone yelling, "Backlog!" When that happens, Ms. Diaz reminds students to pass along notebooks if they're stalled over one story so that everyone can continue to participate in the game.

As the activity continues, Ms. Diaz provides an occasional time cue or checks in to see where everyone is, and she also uses her own progress to determine how much longer everyone needs. When she finishes up a sentence starting with the letter "X" (always a xylophone, it seems), she calls out, "Two more minutes. If you don't get through the entire alphabet, it's okay."

When the round robin has drawn to a close, the time has come to share. "Here is the challenge: Who thinks their story was the most cohesive? That it felt like it was written by the same person, or at least, somewhat close?" Ms. Diaz sits back and observes as four students shoot their hands into the air, while a couple more raise them a little more hesitantly.

"Let's see if the class agrees," she suggests. "For our sharing protocol today, let's put these six stories into one pile here." She indicates a table. "Then, for the stories that you feel have potential but aren't there yet, put them here in this second pile. For the absolutely silly ones, we'll make a third stack right next to them. Take a moment to sort them, please."

Students follow directions and place their stories into the indicated categories on the table. Once everyone settles, Ms. Diaz provides further direction. "These round robin stories are a lot of fun, but they also represent our collective brainpower. Each of us had an equal share in writing the stories in these piles. So, what we're going to do is use our class calling cards to assign readers. We'll start with the first tier of stories, the ones that make the most sense, and work our way out from there."

Having pre-alerted students about the sharing method, Ms. Diaz randomly selects a student to read the first story. The student complies with good nature and everyone is supportive as she reads aloud, interjecting with amused snorts or comments like, "I loved that sentence." At the end, everyone applauds amid laughter and Ms. Diaz shakes her head. "It did hang together, but wow, what a story," she says. "Let's pick our next student to read. We'll keep going until this abbreviated period ends."

When the bell rings a while later, many students groan, and one asks, "Can we finish next time?"

"Maybe," Ms. Diaz says. "We have some other tasks ahead of us, but perhaps we can share a few each day. They are definitely something else!"

As students file out, Ms. Diaz makes neat stacks of the round robin stories, taking care to keep the categories students designed intact and making a separate pile for the ones that were already shared. She will have to think of a way to make time for more students to read them next week.

When students perceive that their classrooms are safe zones, it is because a teacher has gone to careful lengths to ensure that everyone feels confident about their identities as learners in the shared classroom space. In the scenario above, Ms. Diaz takes a number of steps to include each piece of student work and cement its value:

1. She embraces the collective spirit of learning, going so far as to have students create a product that all of them hold equal accountability for producing (herself included).
2. When students are asked to share aloud, the process of selecting student readers is random, transparent, and more inclusive.
3. Ms. Diaz has chosen a low-risk, more engaging assignment for

students to share so that when they are asked to do the same with something more substantial, they will be far more comfortable vocalizing their ideas in a space that has been proven to be supportive.

4. Every student in this classroom has the opportunity and access needed to make their voices heard.

Regardless of the activity or subject matter at hand, building in opportunities for students to showcase their work or ideas when stakes are lower is an important gateway to helping them see their contributions as valid. Then, when more is expected of kids and the work intensifies, they are more likely to rise and meet the expectations of a teacher who clearly believes in their ability to do work that is seen in a positive, productive light.

One element of a classroom that can cause students to feel less safe is how they perceive others feel about them. The damage that labeling can do (inadvertent or otherwise) derails even the most inclusive lesson plans. So, rethinking how students and teachers see one another is a key part of building a safe classroom space. Table 2.4 exemplifies how some common attributes that students either assign one another or themselves come out in dialogue, and suggests ways that teachers can interrupt these stereotypes.

TABLE 2.4

Stereotype Statement	Response
"I never do my work. I'm such a slacker."	"Think about why you hesitate to do your work. What is preventing you from being a more active learner?"
"It's not surprising that he wrote about soccer. He's such a jock."	"It's natural to write about things that interest us, but these interests are not the only factor in defining who we are."
"Only a sci-fi nerd would appreciate this story."	"If a story is engaging, the subject matter is enjoyable for everyone."
"It doesn't matter who raises their hands. The teacher's pets get called on."	"Random calling means that anyone might be asked to contribute a thought. I'm happy to discuss further, but we need to do so after class."

"We're writing about human suffering here. What would a cheerleader know about it?"	"Human experiences are universal. Labeling one another is not kind or productive, nor does it help us learn better."
"Of course they got As. They've all been overachievers since we met in kindergarten."	"Effective effort leads to achievement. We all have the power to get smarter and to learn, but it takes some steps. I'm happy to help."
"Why do teachers always like the popular kids best? I thought they were supposed to be the adults in the room."	"Teachers enjoy talking to ALL students who want to engage productively in class."
"If I like being alone, why can't I work by myself? I've never minded being a loner, so why should you?"	"There is nothing wrong with working alone sometimes, but it is also important to collaborate so that you learn from multiple perspectives."
"I can't share my story; I get too emotional. Everyone says I'm a crier, and it's true."	"Writing is about eliciting emotion from others, so it sounds to me like you're doing something right.

Unfortunately, students will say things that are blatantly hurtful even if their intentions are not malicious, so it is the teacher's job to be ready with a response that invalidates any expressed beliefs that interfere with the desired classroom environment. Then, the restorative work of bringing students together can go from there.

Suppose that a student always declines to work with a group, citing the desire to be alone. When pressed, the student shares, "I do better on my own. Why should I have to work with anyone else? I don't want to."

Without getting into a power struggle with this student, the teacher can provide some choices and redirect the situation by saying, "I'm sorry to hear that you don't feel comfortable working with your peers. How about we come to some agreement about a middle ground? Perhaps we can develop a plan where you work on your own sometimes, but then I ask you to collaborate with others when I think it matters for your learning, and I explain why that is. Is that a compromise you can think about?"

By diffusing the conflict, the teacher in this example has bought some time without giving in to the idea of this student continuing to work alone all the time. Then, the teacher might do some thinking and planning around how to create better connections among the kids in the classroom community. That could involve grouping students strategically or developing more avenues to working together, perhaps with some blended options that incorporate technological tools.

Students enter classrooms with preconceived ideas and identities, but the teacher has the power to exercise positive influence to create a safe zone for learning. When that happens, limitations that have held students back for perhaps their entire school careers will be interrupted, redirected, and forged anew.

Finding the Rose: The Beauty of Participation

Class participation is often viewed as a thorn in everyone's side. Students dislike being forced to speak, or teachers dread the awkwardness of that famed *Ferris Bueller*-style moment: "Anyone, anyone?" We all worry so much about saying too much, too little, the wrong thing, the right thing at the wrong time, the right thing to the wrong person. Does it have to be this stressful?

The short but conditional answer is no. Class participation is complex, but setting up an environment to intentionally include voices in a variety of ways becomes easier as time goes on. When students see our efforts on their behalf, learn to trust us and one another, and enjoy coming into the space we create, the excitement leads to a result that is nothing short of magical. More important, their identities begin to grow and flourish, even beyond school walls.

Cross-Content Strategy

Physical Education, High School
Contributor: Steve McMahon

Context:
In McMahon's school, the physical education (PE) department runs a choice program so students can select an area of PE to work on: net games,

team sports, weight training, yoga, basketball, and soccer. Each student has to earn one credit of PE to graduate, which equates to two semesters.

McMahon teaches net sports (tennis, pickleball, and badminton) which tends to attract students who consider themselves successful academically and highly motivated to succeed. Their focus has historically been on achievement in core content subjects and often they struggle with skillfulness in athletics. Rather than implement one single strategy to build student confidence, McMahon presents a collection of ideas below that work in harmony.

An Ideal Classroom:

McMahon starts each semester with a survey that asks students what they feel is an ideal classroom. The survey includes questions about:

1. Characteristics of an effective teacher
2. Characteristics of an effective student
3. How interactions—teachers–students and students–students— should look

He compiles this information and then the class engages in small group discourse so that students can jointly decide what is most important. The identified characteristics are subsequently posted as classroom tenets. This exercise sets the tone for the semester and shows students that their teacher values their input and that they have a voice. McMahon also gets information about each student as a learner and what they feel is important/effective for their success.

Openness:

McMahon lets students get to know him as he transparently shares the rocky road of how he became a teacher, which includes a history of being on academic probation and almost being expelled from community college. He shares background about his family, relating examples about his own kids and their struggles and successes in school and sports. He talks about not knowing what the right thing to do is, and being scared to make mistakes. Ultimately, McMahon relates the discussion to not allowing anxieties about experiencing failure or doing the wrong thing prevent anyone from taking action. Even flawed action is better than not taking action because it gives us something to build from a starting point. McMahon strongly believes that sharing this explicit perspective pulls back the curtain that many teachers put up in their classes. Students get the clear message that it's not just okay, but ideal to make mistakes.

Celebrating Success:

In PE classes, students are taught to celebrate individual successes, regardless of how small anyone thinks they are. One example could be the level of effort a player is putting forth even when they continue to be beaten in every match they play. While winning is important, the class focuses on factors they can control: effort, sportsmanship, respecting the game, and improving the game. Often, winning is a byproduct of those efforts.

Individualized Plan:

Students are discouraged from comparing themselves to others. Instead, they are asked to compare where they perform currently in relation to where they started or where they were two weeks prior. McMahon always provides a direction or focus that students reflect on and decide to work toward in two-week increments. These must be written down.

The class also completes a brief online self-reflection four times throughout the marking period to identify areas of individual improvement and growth, as exemplified below:

Fill in the three blanks with your self-reflection statements:

1. In the past two weeks, I have improved . . .
2. In the past two weeks, I have learned I need to improve . . .
3. In the next two weeks, I will focus on . . .

Expectations and Assessment:

McMahon holds students to high standards and expectations, which he expresses explicitly and clearly. Students practice meeting criteria for success with daily feedback, and after the first week of school, McMahon and students assess their proficiency with the following:

- Completing all the tasks
- Using correct form
- Using each rep to improve and get better

The warm-up is demonstrated as well as each criteria with examples of positive and delta examples. The warm-up is scaffolded so that each gets more challenging and the skills grow increasingly complex as the class progresses. Class assessments have an element of choice; students know ahead of time when they will be and can choose when they would like to complete them (typically a game concept) in whichever format they decide. Some choose to complete their assessments during the warm-up, some during game play, and others in isolation where it will be a more controlled setting with fewer variables.

In addition, students have an opportunity to reassess. The way McMahon speaks about assessments also makes a difference by referring to them as "opportunities to demonstrate your learning." He tells kids that their goal is to meet criteria correctly and consistently. As such, students know that whether they make a mistake or do it perfectly during the opportunity doesn't matter: Their teacher is evaluating multiple opportunities to determine growth.

CHAPTER 3

Building Student Capacity

Like many high school students, Carrie is attached to her smartphone. Her mother passed away earlier in the year, and the phone is a helpful distraction from what goes on in her real life. Being in school might be a respite from home, but it also seems completely irrelevant most of the time. Her peers are immature, her teachers are always stressed out, and she doesn't feel connected to anything she's learning.

A few weeks ago when Carrie met with Mr. Wu, her school counselor, she didn't object when he signed her up for a composition elective. "You said you like to write," he explained, "and Mr. Hobart's class is the perfect place for that. Kids are usually waitlisted to get into that class, but I talked to him myself about making an exception and he would love to have you. So, you're in."

Whatever, Carrie thought at the time, taking her schedule card from Mr. Wu.

For the past three weeks, Carrie has been sitting in the back of Mr. Hobart's class. She scrolls through her social media feed, pausing only when the teacher is nearby. She dutifully completes her work, giving it the least possible amount of effort before turning back to her phone. So far, Mr. Hobart has been encouraging and friendly, though Carrie can tell he doesn't like her phone being out. Still, he has restrained any criticism, finding nice things to say about her work even though it isn't that great.

It's another Tuesday morning, and Carrie really hates Tuesdays. They're so far from the end of the week. This afternoon, she has to attend therapy after school and make dinner for her dad and little sister before settling into a long evening of homework. She knows she has to live like this, but it's not an existence she enjoys.

As the bell rings, Carrie walks into composition class and slides into her customary back row seat. Most of the kids around her seem happy, chatting about the word on the board: *Thriller*. "What does that mean, Mr. H.?" a boy in the front row asks.

Carrie takes out her phone and begins to scroll as Mr. Hobart gets everyone's attention to start class. "Good question, Nate," he says. "I was going to explain later, but we can talk about it now. Starting this Friday, we're going to do an Open Mic format to share our work. Each week, you'll have a challenge to attempt. This week, we're going to try doing a thriller. I have some samples for us to look at from both classic and popular writers, from Henry James to Dean Koontz."

Despite herself, Carrie feels a stirring of interest. She reads a lot of thrillers, more since losing her mom. They make her feel something, which is a win when so much of the time, a pervasive numbness seems to have taken over her emotions.

Over the next few days, Carrie tries to write the thriller, but she keeps losing interest. It's a lot easier to read suspenseful fiction than to create it herself, and she winds up doing what she always does—phoning it in with a tired, overplayed idea. As she inserts a scary clown into her story, she sighs.

On Friday, the classroom buzz is even more intense than usual. Under the word "Thriller" on the board, Mr. Hobart has also written, "Open Mic Day!" with a little drawing of a microphone. *Cute*, Carrie thinks. She plops herself into her seat and pulls out her phone.

For Open Mic Day, Mr. Hobart has created a sign-up sheet like the kind people use at coffee houses. He has also dimmed the lights, pulled out an actual microphone from somewhere ("my home karaoke machine," he later confides), and borrowed a few couches from the office down the hall. "Let's make this place look a little more inviting," he suggests.

Students pull desks out of the way to make space for the furniture, forming a sort of semicircle around the mic stand. Once everyone is settled, the first student goes up to share his thriller.

Still in the back, Carrie half-listens as she checks her TikTok feed. Nothing new has been posted that she wants to look at, so she closes out the app and pays a little more attention to the boy who is reading his story out loud.

Almost against her will, Carrie starts to feel drawn into the story. She has read a lot of thrillers over the years and is usually immune to being emotionally connected to them, but as the suspense in what the boy narrates starts to build, she feels herself getting nervous. Will the woman in the house make it out? Is she trapped under the bed? And is that noise she hears real, or her imagination? Around her, the class is equally rapt, taking in each word. Gasps and little squeals punctuate the silence from time to time, but otherwise, the tension in the room is palpable.

The boy finishes his story to thunderous applause, and students immediately start reacting. "Wow, I could never write that." "How did you do that?" "That was incredible!"

From her seat, Carrie takes a deep breath. She looks down at her own story, the one she would be too embarrassed to share even before she heard this first offering. Now, she is a little ashamed of her minimal effort, but also strangely inspired. *I know all about thrillers*, she thinks. *I can do this if I just try harder.*

With resolve, she turns her smartphone to "silent" and shoves it deep into the recesses in her backpack. Pulling out her notebook, she starts jotting down ideas for a new thriller before she thinks better of it. She can write a better story later and ask Mr. Hobart to look at it. For now, she wants to hear what other people have written.

In Their Heads

In the constant human pursuit to get inside the heads of others, we sometimes find ourselves asking questions that sound ridiculous: "Are you thinking what I think you're thinking?"

For educators, metacognition has long been a rich area for research and exploration as we seek to uncover what is going through everyone's minds as they learn. In *Making Thinking Visible*, Ron Ritchhart et al. (2011) address the importance of taking time to deconstruct what students perceive: "Uncovering students' thinking gives us evidence of students' insights as well as their misconceptions. We need to make thinking visible because . . . that will take students' learning to the next level and enable continued engagement with the ideas being explored" (p. 27). Unless teachers can see how students make meaning of content, what exactly they understand is questionable. Beneath the acquisition of course concepts, however, lies another layer of student thinking that remains opaque too much of the time, which is how confident they feel about their ability to grow academically.

In Carrie's story at the start of this chapter, her inner life is far more influential to her academic success (or lack thereof) when she first joins Mr. Hobart's class. She has cut herself off from peers and socialization in favor of social media, and it is only when she sees a potentially larger benefit to engaging in her composition class than remaining glued to her phone that she finally decides to make a change. Luckily, Mr. Hobart's class provides just the right kind of environment for Carrie to heal in a supportive learning space and have her work validated.

Making student thinking visible is not just important from the perspective of seeing what kids know, though that matters greatly. It is also vitally important to consider the experiences of everyone in the room as a factor that contributes to their performance. In "Whispering Selves and Reflective Transformations in the Internal Dialogue of Teachers and Students," elementary school teacher Sukhdeep Kaur Chohan (2011) explains that "deeper insights into the inner workings of the classroom can be gained by advancing our understanding of children's and teachers' experiences regarding their inner voice and subsequent interactions in the classroom" (p. 12). Removing the varied experiences that everyone brings to the classroom dynamic is not possible, nor should it be. To build student capacity as learners, we also need to make space for them to grapple with their internal voices.

The challenge of helping students transform what is largely unseen can feel like a wild goose chase if we do not approach the way they think about their own thinking in a specific way. Internal thoughts often go ignored without explicit awareness. For example, I spent many years hating the look of my curly hair, and my inner monologue was hardly flattering. It was only when I realized how that self-talk influenced an overall conception of my appearance that I consciously started to make changes.

I read books about the way American society subversively rejects what is dismissively considered "ethnic" hair, studied ways to get it cut and styled in a way that was far more suitable than the mainstream approaches to straight hair, and began to see my curls as an asset rather than a liability. To get to that point, I needed to intentionally address a deficit mindset and reinvent my perspective.

To that end, teachers do very much the same kind of work when they uncover what goes on inside of their students' heads. Creating the awareness for kids that allows them to rebuild their own perceptions is a first step. To do so, guiding the class through an exploration of mindset while explaining the "why" behind the process must occur before we delve into any other strategies for building student capacity. That way, when students are faced with a series of activities or questions about how they approach learning, they will clearly understand that they are joined with teachers in the mutual goal of figuring out how to make the most of their academic experiences.

Mindset First

It is only the third day of school, and Neil is already feeling overwhelmed. Each new year, he gets his hopes up for no reason. All of his teachers pile on assignments as though their class is the only one he needs to worry about, and he is already staring down several hours of homework. What is the point, anyway? Does he really need to write yet another analytical essay about what the author intends to do with language and find a bunch of examples to support the most boring thesis statement ever? This same essay literally appears every year.

By the time students enter secondary classrooms, they have a well-established set of beliefs about what they expect to learn. However, most of the children we work with are malleable. Teachers have the power to deconstruct less productive beliefs and build a different mindset, but this process only occurs through being explicit about how our classes will adjust established norms. Mindsets are notoriously challenging to shift, and the process cannot be undertaken without being very clear about what we hope to achieve.

In *Teach More, Hover Less* (2022), I outline the first stage of implementing "hover-free" instruction, which is centered on shifting teacher mindset to address belief around student capacity. This complex challenge involves "the process of changing our own minds and learning to see what we previously held as truth in a completely different light" (p. 14). Through a series of tools intended to create reflection around beliefs, the book guides readers through questioning their own deep-seated assumptions about teaching and learning. By explicitly asking ourselves if we micromanage our classrooms, we increase our awareness around habits that might need to shift.

Students can undergo the same type of guidance with the help of trusted, skillful teachers. The quiz in Box 3.1 allows students to reflect upon their beliefs about learning in an accessible, familiar way. Mimicking the kinds of quizzes found in magazines or online feeds, this method of self-assessment is both engaging and quick.

BOX 3.1

Directions: Circle the answer that most closely describes your beliefs about learning.

Question 1

When I walk into class each day, my assumption is most often that:

A. I will be interested and engaged in what is happening.
B. Whatever we do will be boring.
C. Maybe this class will be a good one, but it changes from day to day.

Question 2

If my teacher asks the class a question:

D. I raise my hand if I think I know the answer.
E. I try my best not to make eye contact because I don't want to be called on.
F. Occasionally I will raise my hand, but only if the kids who normally get called on don't put their hands up or if I'm absolutely positive I know the answer.

Question 3

When it comes to my academic achievement:

A. I see myself as a good student and a high achiever.
B. I'm not someone who enjoys school or does well in class.
C. Some subjects are fine, but there are also some subjects I'm not as good at.

Question 4

If my teacher asks me to share something I wrote:

A. It doesn't make me self-conscious to share my work most of the time.
B. I really don't want anyone to see what I write.
C. There are some kinds of writing I don't mind sharing, but I don't want people to see it most of the time.

Question 5

The person who is most responsible for my learning is:

A. Mainly me
B. Both my teacher and me
C. Mainly the teacher

The quiz in Box 3.1 is for students to complete privately and is most effective when they engage in self-assessment by analyzing their own responses. Teachers may choose to point out the possible significance of certain patterns even though they are fairly clear, especially to older learners. Students who circle mostly "A" answers are likely to perceive themselves as high achievers who are responsible for their own academic success or failure. Conversely, students who opt to circle "B" for a majority of their responses may feel uncomfortable in classroom settings and perceive that they lack control over their own learning process. Those who respond with a large number of "Cs" occupy more of a middle ground, attributing their performance in any given class to the circumstances that exist in each space. For students whose answers do not follow a particular pattern, they can be directed to look at their responses one by one to determine why their classroom history represents a wider range of possible associations or experiences.

However students choose to reflect upon the results on this informal quiz, they might notice that for every class in which they are enrolled, the answers to the quiz questions diverge. In that case, their learning is more dependent on external factors (i.e., the teacher, students, and space around them) than on their internal sense of academic identity. The more answers on the quiz might vary from class to class, the less secure students feel in their ability to manage their own learning.

To combat what seems like stronger forces around them that determine success or failure, the next step to building student mindset is focusing the work of identity inward so that the inner voice of learned helplessness can transform into a far more empowering influence. Table 3.1 presents a strategy for confronting the less helpful thoughts students harbor about themselves, and then asks them to embrace a more favorable perspective.

TABLE 3.1

Thoughts About Myself	Flip It!
These books are so incredibly boring. I hate reading.	I don't enjoy reading in class, but I like reading at home.
For the most part, I'm a bad student. I can't wait to get out of here.	When I'm interested in something, I do better at it.
Nobody wants to hear what I have to say, so I keep my mouth shut.	My friends like talking to me, so maybe I do say some good things sometimes.
My teachers don't like me. They're always telling me I can do more.	It's possible that my teachers are frustrated, but that they have nothing against me.
What I just wrote is really horrible. I hope nobody reads it.	This needs some work, but it can get better if I work on it.
School isn't my happy place. I like lunchtime, and that's about it.	When my friends are in class with me, I don't mind being in school.

Thoughts About Myself	Flip It!
This teacher is terrible, so I won't be learning anything here.	What I learn does not always have to depend on what the teacher does.
Some kids seem so happy to be here. I wonder what's wrong with me.	If I'm comfortable, I'm happier. What can I do to feel better in this space?

In Table 3.1, students face a difficult task. Recording feelings in writing about themselves can be a scary thing to do, and many will be nervous about putting anything so personal on paper. As is the case with Box 3.1, teachers must stress to students before they embark upon this activity that it is personal, and not meant to be shared. When students have worked on their charts, teachers may invite them to take a picture on their phones and rip up the original, or just do the latter without capturing the photo. Those who are less concerned are welcome to keep their charts, but no matter what, nobody should be asked to share what they did. The teacher can offer to discuss the charts privately with anyone who wishes to have that conversation, but that is as far as this activity should go. Otherwise, the trust that we so carefully work to build will be breached.

If there is a concern that students will try to look at one another's work for Box 3.1 and Table 3.1, it makes more sense to assign this work at home to be done privately, and then ask students to reflect upon one thing they discovered about themselves within the space of the classroom. The aspiration of a safe, low-risk academic environment is a desired state well worth striving for, but it cannot always be established immediately. Sometimes, classroom chemistry is more complicated.

Only when students have begun to consider their mindsets can teachers move to the next phase of building capacity by changing the narrative around how students see themselves. Then, when students feel as though they are being underestimated in any classroom space, they are more likely to have the inner strength to speak out and confront any misconceptions about how they learn.

Changing the Narrative

Greta looks down at the returned assignment in her hands, confused. On the top of the page is the B grade she typically receives, and ordinarily, that is not something she takes issue with. She has never considered herself a high achiever; she saves that for her older brother, Sam. Whenever Greta gets teachers who also had Sam, they almost never fail to rave about how much they loved having him in class, how smart he is, and how excited they are to have another member of the family. That is, until they realize she is not anything like Sam.

For her entire academic life, Greta has been a decent student. She is cooperative in class but not enthusiastic, does her work (but only what is required of her and not beyond), and earns grades that are fair to good. It's not that she aims for mediocrity, but school has never been her thing. She loves sports, and she spends most of her happy hours outside with friends shooting hoops or playing on school teams. She also enjoys having a social life, something that Sam never really embraced with quite the vigor that Greta does. If she has to choose between just doing fine in school and having fun on evenings and weekends or being a straight-A student, she knows exactly what the best pathway is for her.

Having said that, Greta gets excited about certain assignments, which is why the B in front of her is befuddling. Last week, her 11th-grade English teacher assigned a satire for homework in preparation for a unit on humor. Greta loves reading funny things and she got very into writing her own satire, choosing to make fun of the constant disrepair in their worn-down school building by blowing the situation way out of proportion. Unlike some of the other essays she has written for class, this one seemed effortless as words flew across the page. When she turned in the assignment, she couldn't wait to see what her teacher thought.

And now, there it is—the usual B emblazoned atop the page. Other than a check mark, there are no comments or feedback on any of the pages. Greta starts to do what she usually does, which is to stuff her paper far into the recesses of her jumbled backpack. But as the pages make contact with the Twinkie she packed for a snack (so disgusting, yet so wonderful), something stops Greta from pushing the assignment down any further. Glancing toward the teacher's desk, she sees that Ms. Myles is alone.

Greta squares her shoulders and heads to the front of the room. "Ms. Myles? Do you have a second?"

Her teacher looks up from her computer. "Of course, Greta. What's up?"

"It's my paper," Greta says, showing it to her. "You see, I know I get Bs a lot in this class, and I'm not the best writer. But I felt different about this assignment. I was really excited to write it, and I honestly thought it was better than this. What did I do wrong?"

Ms. Myles is a little surprised to see Greta at her desk. She would have expected Sam to come to her with questions, but Greta seems to be fairly blasé about school. She is friendly enough, but doesn't have the open, engaged demeanor that made teaching Sam such a pleasure.

Holding out her hand for the paper, Ms. Myles asks, "Can I see?"

Ms. Myles scans it, reminding herself of what she read the first time, and realizes that the night she graded Greta's paper was the same evening her tire went flat. She'd spent far too much time at the gas station, trying to read the assignments while waiting for her car to be ready. As she looks at Greta's paper again, Ms. Myles realizes she may have assigned the grade this student always seems to get without reading carefully, figuring it was more of the same.

As shame seeps in, Ms. Myles looks at Greta. "Is it okay if I hold onto this tonight? I just need a little more time."

Greta seems taken aback, but she nods, picking up her backpack to head to her next class. "Sure."

The next day, Ms. Myles intercepts Greta on her way into class. "Do you have time to see me at lunch today?"

Greta is instantly apprehensive. "Is this about my paper?"

"Yes, but nothing to worry about. I just wanted us to have time to talk in private. All good things, I promise."

Later that day, Greta walks into the English office with hesitation. She has never been in this space before, and she is intimidated to see some of her former teachers laughing, kicking back, and eating lunch. Mr. Fitch, her teacher from last year, spies her. "Greta! What can we do for you?"

"I'm looking for Ms. Myles," she says.

"Back row," he says, pointing at a line of desks. "Good to see you, kiddo."

She smiles at him. Mr. Fitch was always nice to her.

Ms. Myles is sitting at a desk, and she beckons Greta over when she sees her.

"Pull up a chair," she instructs. "Did you bring something to eat? I don't want you to miss lunch."

"Oh." Greta would rather not eat in front of her teacher, but she doesn't want to seem contrary. She pulls out her package of Twinkies.

Ms. Myles eyes the Twinkies. "No, ma'am. That cannot be your lunch."

"I'm more of a snacker," Greta says, embarrassed.

"Put that away," Ms. Myles says, reaching into her desk drawer. "That's all very well and good for a snack, but here. What would you like?" She holds out a variety of protein bars in different flavors and some little bags of carrots. "These have some nutrients in them to see you through."

Surprised but a little touched, Greta picks a chocolate chip flavored bar. "Can't help it," she explains. "I really love sweet things."

"Me too, if I'm being honest. Now," says Ms. Myles, taking a deep breath. "Your paper." She pulls it out. "The reason I asked you to come to my office is that I owe you a huge apology. I did something I promised myself I would never do, and I did it with your paper. I could tell you with absolute truth that it was unintentional, but that doesn't make it any less hurtful."

Greta shakes her head. "I don't understand."

"On the day I graded your paper, my tire went flat on the way home. To make a long story short, I was waiting for it to be ready and grading at the same time, and I was so distracted that I didn't read your paper carefully. At best, I skimmed it. And the grade I gave you . . . well, this is hard to say, but I wasn't fair to you."

Reading between the lines, Greta says, "You gave me the grade you always gave me. You figured it was a safe thing to do."

Ms. Myles nods. "And what a horrible thing that was for me to do. I take full responsibility, and I am truly ashamed of myself. I don't know why any part of me decided it was okay to look at your work that way, and I intend to hold myself accountable to the entire class and apologize for what happened."

Alarmed, Greta breaks in. "Please don't tell them about this, Ms. Myles. I don't want to be held up as an example or whatever."

"No, no," Ms. Myles assures her. "I won't mention any names. I'll just explain what happened, say that I never intended to disregard anyone's work, and ask everyone to resubmit their papers so that I can look at them properly. If I graded anyone too highly, I won't change that. I just want to fix the papers I underestimated. And boy, did I ever underestimate yours." She hands Greta her satire.

On the top of the page, Greta sees an "A+" written in Sharpie. For a split second, she feels joyful. Then, doubt creeps back in. "Is this really that good, or are you just being nice because you feel bad? Because I don't want a grade I didn't earn."

"This is what I was afraid of. It's my fault you don't believe me. Your satire is top-notch, one of the better ones I've read over the many years of grading this assignment. It's so good that I'd like your permission to submit it to our school's literary magazine."

"Really? Are you sure? Because—" Greta stops herself.

"Because what? Spill."

"Because," Greta says, her face growing red. "Writing has always been Sam's thing."

Ms. Myles looks at the girl in front of her, the one she has felt disappointed in so many times in the past, and a curtain suddenly lifts. It must be so hard to spend her entire life being compared to someone unfavorably, especially when she has gifts that nobody chooses to see. Ms. Myles should know. After all, her younger sister always stole the spotlight, and nobody paid much attention to what her older, more hardworking sister was doing.

"If you write," Ms. Myles tells Greta, "you are a writer. That's all it takes. And as you have shown both me and yourself, you are formidable when you choose to put forth the effort and when you believe in yourself. Forget about Sam. This is about you."

Slowly, a grin forms across Greta's face, lighting her up from within. "You know what, Ms. Myles? Forgetting Sam is hard, but I'll try. If you think I have something worthwhile to share, I mean."

"You really do," Ms. Myles says. "And I'm taking this satire back again so we can get it entered in the running for publication. Sound good?"

"Absolutely," Greta says.

"Now, I have an apology to brainstorm and you have those Twinkies waiting for you," Ms. Myles says. "But I have one more question before I let you go. What made you come up to me and tell me the paper was better than a B?"

"I've been wondering that myself," Greta admits. "I guess it's that I'm used to being just kind of okay at things, and not caring much about so many assignments. But that one, I really loved. And when I saw that B . . . it's almost like something snapped. I knew it was better."

"You were right," Ms. Myles says. "And I can't tell you how much I respect you for your strength, and by sticking with your own convictions about yourself. I'm learning so much from you."

"Thanks," Greta says. She leans over and picks up her backpack.

"Off you go," Ms. Myles says. "And take some carrots for the road. You need vitamins."

"Okay," Greta says, laughing. As she leaves the office, she feels like an entirely different person. She can't wait for English class, either. Ms. Myles might be her new favorite teacher.

Intentionally or not, many students are conditioned to be self-deprecating. As a result, the narrative they hold around their own academic worth is negatively influenced by a world that tells them to consider their capacity inferior to the adults who teach them. By directly addressing this prevailing mindset to change the narrative and build confidence, students do not have to experience the same dissonance that finally drives Greta to confront her teacher, or worse, be too intimidated to ever stand up for themselves. Once students have shifted their mindsets to the point that they are open to looking at themselves as valuable members of the classroom community, their emerging beliefs must be reinforced in the way the classes function.

To dig further into the exploration of self in connection with academic identity, students benefit from looking into who they have been as learners, and who they would like to become. Instead of asking the class to look forward from their current vantage point, one creative exercise that builds awareness about the concept of a "future self" is featured in Box 3.2 in the form of a letter.

BOX 3.2

Future Self Letter

DIRECTIONS:

Imagine a future version of yourself, one that you have worked hard to become over the years.

Write yourself a letter from this older person's perspective. As you write, envision how the experiences of this future self can provide advice or counsel to help your present self.

In the world your future self inhabits, current realities need not apply. You can invent technological advancements, time travel, journeys to other galaxies, and so forth. There is no need to feel constrained by the world we live in now.

You are encouraged to have fun with this, to be creative, and to not take it overly seriously. Still, make sure the core of what you write is sincere, and that you address some of what your current self worries about with wisdom from your future self.

When teachers guide students through writing "future self" letters, the directions can be tweaked for more specific purposes. For example, in a science class, the teacher may wish students to imagine future innovations that bridge from a unit of study; or in math, the teacher might ask everyone to predict how a specific skill might come in useful down the road. The template in Box 3.2 provides a place to begin, but can be adapted for a variety of needs and content area approaches.

However individual teachers or teams might choose to approach the activity in Box 3.2, the objective remains the same: build student awareness around their own capacity. It's difficult for anyone to imagine life beyond the present moment, and that is especially true for younger learners who have fewer experiences to draw from. When faced with the "someday" vision of themselves in a more concrete way, preteens and teens see the larger focus of who they may become.

To further the process of altering a potentially deficit mindset narrative students have been living with for the majority of their lives, the idea of change can become more actionable. In Box 3.3, students are asked to think about just one thing they might change about their academic lives to take a productive step forward.

BOX 3.3

One Thing to Change

DIRECTIONS:

We all feel good at some things, and less skilled at others. That's called being human.

Of the difficulties you face in school, what might be getting in the way of your learning the most?

Identify **one** area for change this year. It can be something small, like packing your backpack the night before each school day with needed supplies, or something bigger, like working on a specific study skill to improve your performance in a class.

You can respond in anywhere from a few sentences to a paragraph. Be as detailed as possible. If desired, you can include action steps or a timeline.

When students are asked to do too much, the cognitive overload may result in a total shutdown of any desire to complete a task. When work is divided into manageable chunks, however, kids are far more likely to engage with what teachers ask for. In the activity featured in Box 3.3, students are encouraged to think of just one action to achieve their academic goals, regardless of whether the scope is larger or smaller. Helping kids realize that little changes make a huge impact is an important lesson, and often an enlightening one.

The follow-through for students who engage in activities like the ones featured in Boxes 3.2 and 3.3 is to discuss how what they wrote contributes to altering their perspective around who they are now, and who they will become. We all have the power to be the best versions of ourselves; nobody should stand in the way of that. Teachers may hold onto the future self letters and redistribute them at the end of the year for reflection, and they can collect the "one thing" ideas and brainstorm ways to help each student meet identified goals. Once we begin the process of helping students change their narratives, the journey must continue with a dogged determination to help kids see the good in themselves as learners, thinkers, and scholars.

Writing Practices for Capacity-Building

In *The Cat in the Hat* by Dr. Seuss (1957), the seemingly unhinged yet wise titular character says to the children whose house he has invaded: "It's fun to have fun, but you have to know how" (p. 18). In recent years, teachers have increasingly gamified instruction to meet a growing need to make learning more appealing. While online applications and tools provide plenty of avenues for the gamification route, technology is not a non-negotiable part of connecting content goals to enjoyable processes. If teachers know how to have fun in a way that explicitly promotes student learning, everyone wins.

Not to knock gamification, but students can also enjoy the work they do without having that aspect of competition or a video game-style presentation. Writing activities that do not rely on technological tools have the added benefit of being able to be executed in a variety of ways, from any location. The more open assignments can be, the more students are able to tap into higher-order thinking skills to create products that excite them. As an example, the open-ended assignment featured in Box 3.4 is a nice option to offer students periodically throughout the year. Sometimes, the complete openness of the guidelines intimidates certain students who have not been accustomed to taking risks in previous classes, but with a clearly outlined brainstorming process and a strong classroom community as a support system, the engagement that follows from having a wide degree of choice is formidable.

BOX 3.4

Open-Ended Piece:
An Independent (Supervised) Writing Journey

What do you really want to write? This time, it's up to you. The possibilities are endless. Really test your creative boundaries. Do something
you've never done before! Take a risk, even if it doesn't work out the way
you hoped for.

Your choices include:

- Chapter from a novel you're working/wanting to work on
- Short story in any genre (or mix of genres) on any topic
- Collection of poetry
- Short play, screenplay, or monologue
- Chapter from a graphic novel/novella
- Children's book
- Work of nonfiction
- Whatever else: you name it!

Even though mechanics is not the main focus in this class, please make
sure your final drafts are polished and well-edited. It's important to make
the best possible impression!

And remember: it's all about getting that good idea, having some ingenuity. So PLEASE take the brainstorming process seriously.

This project will be due on [insert date here].

A clear benefit of the assignment described in Box 3.4 is that teachers learn
so much more about students when they offer this choice-based approach
to writing. If all classroom assignments are teacher-directed in every way,
individuals who produce good work that doesn't fall within the traditional
confines of class content never get to exhibit their strengths. By allowing
students to drive their own work from time to time, teachers are able to
see skills that would otherwise remain under the surface. Then, with new
knowledge about what everyone can do, it becomes easier to take more
targeted steps to build capacity with specific information about how to
move forward.

When teachers create a space that welcomes all voices for the purpose of bolstering how students see themselves, considering the role of praise in the classroom is important. If mishandled, praise can be more destructive than productive. In "How Not to Talk to Your Kids," writer Po Bronson (2007) summarizes thoughts from education researcher Carol Dweck and her team about the harm that praising kids can ultimately cause in how children perceive their academic capacity: "Dweck discovered that those who think that innate intelligence is the key to success begin to discount the importance of effort." Essentially, when kids are liberally praised for being "smart," they attribute less of their success or failure to making an effective effort toward achievement. This fixed mindset approach damages how students perceive themselves, and if left uncorrected, the effects can be lasting.

However, praise has a place. As Bronson explains: "But all praise is not equal—and, as Dweck demonstrated, the effects of praise can vary significantly depending on the praise given. To be effective, researchers have found, praise needs to be specific." When teachers find particular aspects of student work to applaud, and when they focus on effort and hard work rather than innate ability, praise is far more useful. Bronson also adds that praise must be sincere, which means that any vague comments along the lines of "good work" or "nicely done" do nothing to help students grow in their learning or in their sense of intelligence.

Beyond the way that teachers praise students, it is also important to show them how to recognize one another in ways that are substantive, not shallow. To that end, Table 3.2 exemplifies a two-pronged constructive criticism method that includes a space for peers to provide one another with thoughts that encompass both areas for improvement (the "specific suggestions") and meaningful praise (the "warm fuzzies"). As students look at one another's work, they fill in a chart with ideas for each category. This activity could be something students do one-on-one as they engage in peer review, or individuals could move from desk to desk and write on a copy of the chart that is attached to each piece of peer work. Either way, it is advisable for all students to include their names next to what they write, both for follow-up purposes and to increase a sense of community. Table 3.2 shares a few sample entries for each category to model the process.

TABLE 3.2

Warm Fuzzies	Specific Suggestions
Your descriptions are so vivid! I could almost taste the cupcake the girl was eating.	Adding dialogue might be a good way to change things up a little.
The characters are really clearly sketched out, like I know them.	There are a few minor mechanics tweaks, so I circled them for you.
Where did you come up with this idea? It's so original!	I wasn't sure why Johnny left the group at the beginning.
It is clear that you really love your setting. I felt like I was there with you.	There are some references that might be hard for people to get. I circled them!

Too often, students only experience negative comments from teachers on their work. A lot of this less ideal reality is born of being in a hurry; it can be hard to find time to highlight what is good about an assignment as well as what needs improvement. When students are taught to be analytical with one another about isolating what works well, teachers model a process that we would do well to emulate ourselves. That way, when anyone sets out to bolster student self-perception, they do so in a way that clearly communicates the message that each student always has something of value to share, no matter what.

The Beauty of Capacity

On the face of it, the word "capacity" doesn't sound glamorous. It brings associations to mind like making an unwieldy bag fit into the overhead bin on an airplane. In the case of academics, capacity usually refers to what students can achieve. This concept cannot be a fixed point, so teachers must present capacity as an area of continuous growth. By highlighting the power of everyone in the room to strengthen their ability each day with a variety of approaches that build awareness and confidence, teachers can finally show students that their worth is significant, and that they can increase their capacity each day as they build an identity that grows beyond a classroom space.

Cross-Content Strategy

English Language Arts, High School

Contributor: Miriam Plotinsky

While writing-centric strategies are plentiful throughout this book, those that overtly tie into English Language Arts (ELA) content have not been the sole focus. In the ELA sphere, reading instruction goes hand in hand with writing as two of the largest language domains. To demonstrate how teachers can build text comprehension in a way that also cements student confidence, the following activity is one I used with my students for many years to connect their background knowledge to a genre that can be intimidating to read and even scarier to talk about in a larger group: poetry.

The purpose of this featured lesson is not just to make poetry more accessible, but also to help students grow their confidence about analyzing rhetoric by looking beyond the medium of writing. In school, kids are accustomed to either interpreting persuasive essays or writing their own. For this project, the goal is to help them connect to what Aristotle called "the art of persuasion" in a visual medium.

Here is the series of slides students are given access to throughout instruction as a resource and guide:

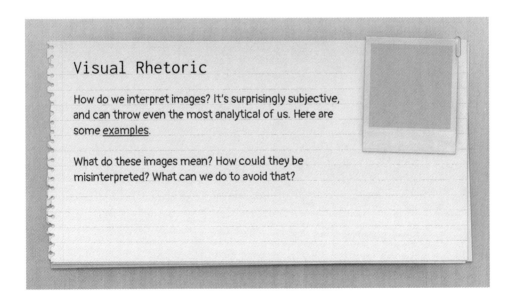

Visual Rhetoric

How do we interpret images? It's surprisingly subjective, and can throw even the most analytical of us. Here are some examples.

What do these images mean? How could they be misinterpreted? What can we do to avoid that?

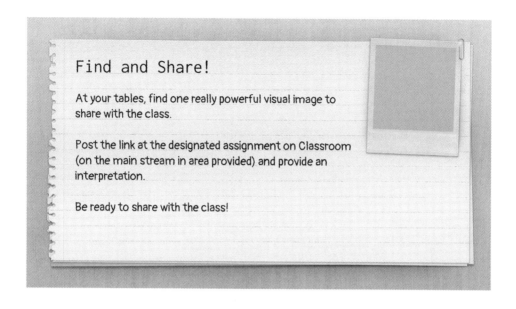

Bearing in mind the continuing goal to maintain academic identity, the lesson featured above has a purposeful approach for what can best be described as, "accessible entry, high expectations." In other words, by starting with the idea of interpreting images rather than dense text, all students are more comfortable taking part in the learning.

As students scroll through the images in table groups, they look for the overt or implied persuasive message of the visual they see, also considering possible misinterpretations. The next step, as explained on the following slide, is to collaborate by selecting a powerful visual from the web and interpret the image's message for the rest of the class. The benefits of this portion of the activity are numerous. Students are given the power to choose what images they analyze, and they are also permitted to work together, which minimizes any feeling of risk at being considered "wrong" when approaching a newer concept. In addition, the cognitive process of determining a hidden argument within a visual image is more accessible with self-selected pictures, preparing the class for a series of more challenging texts (both visual and written) in the following slide.

Once students have practiced interpreting visuals that are more accessible, the class moves into something a little more rigorous, which is the examination of Peter Bruegel's Renaissance painting *The Fall of Icarus* in conjunction with the poem "Musee des Beaux Arts" by W. H. Auden. First, the class looks carefully at the painting, trying to find an "Easter egg" of sorts. Usually, at least one student will notice the odd image of a pair of legs flailing in the sea in the painting's foreground. Some students might know the mythological story of Icarus and be able to fill in their classmates, or some additional scaffolding might be needed to make the painting's allusion clear.

Either way, when it comes time to read Auden's poem, his reference to the painting makes sense and the poem is generally more accessible for students in terms of comprehension than it would have been without the background context. From there, the conversation becomes focused once again on rhetoric. What is Bruegel's purpose in the image he painted? And for Auden, what message is he trying to relay?

Regardless of the specific texts (visual or written) that teachers choose to select in helping students more deeply understand what they look at, this activity is easily replicated with any number of pictures, poems, or readings across the secondary grades. The purpose of an exercise like this one is to build student belief in their capacity to interpret a variety of resources by allowing them some degree of choice, added access and a risk-free collectivist space to share ideas. That way, when they encounter increasingly complex and challenging texts, students will feel more prepared to meet the task head-on, seeing themselves as capable learners with strategies in their toolboxes.

Feedback and Identity

The Feedback Hole

"I'm passing back your essays," Dr. Benson announces. "The grade is at the top, and I added holistic comments on the last page for everyone."

Will sinks down a little lower in his seat. He doesn't want to see his grade; he rarely does. *I wonder what "holistic" means*, he thinks, not raising his hand to ask. Will's eyes track his classmates as their papers are returned, noting the range of reactions. He might feel something when he sees his paper, but he won't be visibly reacting to anything.

Dr. Benson is suddenly in front of Will, holding out the assignment. "Here you go," Dr. Benson says, his voice neutral. "Let me know if you have questions."

Taking the paper, Will takes a quick look and sees a large "C" written in purple ink. Sighing, he flips briefly through the pages until he comes to a long, written comment at the end. The handwriting is difficult to parse out and instead of struggling with it, Will folds up the paper and sticks it in a folder. *Maybe I'll read it later*, he thinks. He knows he probably won't.

At the front of the room, Dr. Benson sees Will put the paper away without taking the time to read his comments on the last page and tries to mask his anger. All that time grading, and so few students so much as

glance at what he writes to them. Hours of work wasted and unappreci-
ated. Why should he even bother?

Welcome to what may as well be called the "feedback hole." Nearly
every teacher alive has experienced the frustration Dr. Benson feels,
and nearly every student to ever grace a traditional education setting
can relate to Will. Teachers expend an enormous amount of time and
effort marking up papers, only to watch students ignore their suggestions.
For their part, students find grades to be perplexing, even with written explanations. Thus, a vicious cycle perpetuates itself in classrooms
as teachers wonder why students ignore feedback that could help them
improve, while students do not truly understand how to interpret what
teachers communicate.

The role of feedback in building student academic identity is significant. If students do not feel as though their achievement is a movable
entity, they remain stuck in one area of performance and conclude that
they are not competent learners. Too much of the time, teachers uninten-
tionally pollute what should be an objective, value-free feedback process
with judgmental or biased information that is both confusing and discouraging. To fill in the hole once and for all, the first step to becoming more
effective with feedback lies in understanding its true purpose.

Feedback, Guidance, Evaluation

When teachers hand back student work, the air in a classroom shifts. One
by one, students pick up their papers, look at their grades, and if given the
leeway, start comparing their results. Whether vocalized or not, students
thinking might occur along these lines:

- "I thought I did better than this."
- "Bombed it. As usual."
- "I don't understand. How did I do so well? I didn't even try."
- "I actually studied. Guess it didn't make any difference."
- "Easy A. This teacher is boring, but at least I know what to expect."

And so forth. From the moment we are born, we start looking for ways
to explain the results of our efforts, be they personal or otherwise. In

1958, psychologist Fritz Heider defined what is commonly known as attribution theory to explain how individuals make sense of their own success or failure. From an education standpoint, both teachers and students tend to explain performance on tasks through a series of possible causal misattributions.

To illustrate this idea, I think of my high school physics class. In twelfth grade, I struggled to be successful in physics (a required course for graduation), often resorting to doing a large number of extra credit assignments to eke out a mediocre grade. My test grades in particular were abysmal, with one notable exception. Somewhere in the middle of the year, we had a shorter assessment that exemplified what teachers sometimes call a series of "plug and chug" formula-based mathematical problems. The one I remember to this day is that force equals mass times acceleration, but there were a number of similar formulas on that one test.

At the time, I was a decent student, and I had dutifully studied my formulas in the weeks preceding the class. If asked, I could not have explained much about what exactly force or mass were, but I knew where the numbers were supposed to go.

On the day we received our test scores, my physics teacher walked up to me, beaming. "Look at that," he exclaimed, giving me the paper. "What a great improvement!"

Sure enough, I had earned an A for the first time that year, and my momentary joy was followed quickly by another thought. *Well, duh. This test was based on easy stuff. I just got lucky.*

When my next physics test resulted in the usual low score, any conclusions about why I had been successful that one time were fully cemented. A factor outside my control—happy chance, to be exact—had earned me that high grade. My own success could be attributed only to that, and I continued to consider myself a weak student of physics.

Researchers point out that correlation does not equal causation, which is a piece of wisdom teachers would do well to consider when we try to determine why some students achieve more than others. In 1972, education professor Bernard Weiner analyzed how flawed our perceptions can be: "Inasmuch as perceptions of causality influence the affect experienced in achievement-oriented activities, one's causal biases when interpreting success or failure have important implications for achievement striving" (p. 206). While one might hope that anyone's ability guides their academic success, the reality is that the idea of achievement is up to interpretation, or in too many cases, misinterpretation.

Even putting aside the opinions teachers may hold (consciously or not) of what students are able to do, children are not yet equipped to accurately judge their own ability without knowledgeable adult guidance. When it comes to determining self-worth, most people are their own worst enemies. If preteens and teens—already not the most confident group—receive information from adults that negates their sense of academic competence, they will believe from a very young age that they are poor students, underachievers, or just plain stupid. That is why so many students dread being graded, and why the entire process remains a loaded one.

While part of the human experience is to walk around feeling judged, it is possible to ease much of the burden associated with feedback for both teachers and students. The first step to creating a more functional classroom environment around the assessment process is rooted in determining what exactly it means to provide feedback so that the purpose of sharing it with students is not misconstrued.

To begin, the word "feedback" needs to be properly defined to be implemented as intended. In "Seven Keys to Effective Feedback," education researcher Grant Wiggins (2013) delineates the differences among three commonly confused entities. He writes: "The term feedback is often used to describe all kinds of comments made after the fact, including advice, praise, and evaluation. But none of these are feedback, strictly speaking" (p. 1). When teachers grade papers, they conflate these categories into the general umbrella of feedback, leading students to believe that the process of assessing their work is subjective. As a result, students are more apt to disregard anything a teacher tells them about their work, especially if they think the teacher does not like or trust them.

The best way to combat this belief about biased feedback and build additional trust with students is to change the way the entire process is presented. First and foremost, teachers must make it clear in no uncertain terms that feedback is provided in relation to an identified learning outcome. In *Edutopia* article "3 Strategies to Reduce Student Burnout," I provide an example of what it looks like to give objective feedback for a specific target:

> For example, if a class is assigned a paragraph of between five and eight sentences to write, and a student writes only three sentences, the teacher can provide the neutral feedback that the paragraph is shorter than the stated expectation for the product. However, many teachers confuse feedback for either guidance or evaluation. In the first case, that might look like a suggestion (e.g., "You need to write more and include details"), and in the second, a judgment-based response (like a letter grade or a "Getting there!"). (Plotinsky, 2022)

In the example above, students have been given a very specific set of criteria that determines their success. When teachers give feedback, they indicate whether the student meets criteria as defined by the provided expectation, and this happens in a manner that is free of judgment or value. Students should not be shamed for not writing the requisite number of sentences; instead, they are shown where they currently stand based upon stated criteria and what must be done to improve their performance. If the teacher wishes to provide guidance to help them along, there is nothing wrong with that. However, that should be done in a separate area, either on the assignment itself or in a verbal communication, and the same holds true for evaluative information.

To demonstrate what this process looks like, consider the sample provided in Box 4.1 as a possible model for improving feedback. In this example, the teacher has placed clear criteria for success on the assignment, checking off what Kelly, the student, has achieved and indicating what she has yet to accomplish. Then, the guidance and evaluation follow in a separate area to increase clarity for Kelly about her next steps.

Ideally, criteria for success should be included as part of an assignment at the outset upon giving students the work. That way, the necessary steps to be successful are transparent from the start, resulting in what many educators refer to as a "no-secrets" classroom. Otherwise, the idea of success remains elusive to students and learning is perceived as more of a puzzle or a "gotcha," leading to pervasive distrust of the teacher and

BOX 4.1

Assignment Feedback, Persuasive Paragraph

Name: Kelly T.

CRITERIA FOR SUCCESS (CFS):

☐ You have written between three and five sentences.

✓ The document is spell-checked.

✓ The paragraph includes a topic sentence that makes a clear persuasive point.

☐ One relevant example from the book (either a paraphrase or a quotation) has been inserted as support and cited properly.

☐ You have explained how the example supports the topic sentence.

GUIDANCE:

Kelly, thanks for starting this! To improve your grade (see "Evaluation" below), my suggestion is that you make two specific edits:

1. So far, your paragraph has only two sentences. Per our CFS, you need at least three. I'm happy to help if you're stuck.

2. As the CFS states, you need a cited example from the book to support your topic sentence. Please include that to support your ideas, and then you will also have successfully provided an explanation that ties your ideas together.

EVALUATION:

Exceeds Criteria	Meets Criteria	Not Yet
		So far, the paragraph has *not yet* met the criteria for success, so the current grade is at a "1" on our 0–5 rubric.

with it, a lower sense of academic credibility. If kids can't figure out what the teacher wants, after all, perhaps it is their fault. Adults have an ethos that children do not, and a feedback process that is perceived as biased can become a burden that students take upon themselves when they experience too much failure.

If we want to internalize this messaging from the teacher's vantage point of delivering instruction, think about the feedback that supervisors have provided in the past during classroom observation. Wiggins (2013) provides an exceedingly relatable example:

> Many so-called feedback situations lead to arguments because the givers are not sufficiently descriptive; they jump to an inference from the data instead of simply presenting the data. For example, a supervisor may make the unfortunate but common mistake of stating that "many students were bored in class." That's a judgment, not an observation. It would have been far more useful and less debatable had the supervisor said something like, "I counted ongoing inattentive behaviors in 12 of the 25 students once the lecture was underway. The behaviors included texting under desks, passing notes, and making eye contact with other students. However, after the small-group exercise began, I saw such behavior in only one student." (p. 5)

Just like their students, teachers need objective information about where instruction sits in relation to a goal. Otherwise, just like the grading process, classroom observation becomes a dreaded experience that is unfair and tainted by bias.

To make the distinction between feedback and its impostors absolutely clear, Table 4.1 is a quick-reference chart that identifies what true feedback looks like, and what muddies the waters for everyone.

TABLE 4.1

Feedback Is . . .	Feedback Is Not . . .
Actionable	Inapplicable
Direct and concise	Long-winded and elusive
Written for student understanding	Jargon
Focused on student work	Focused on student habits or behavior
Based on fact	Judgmental or evaluative

Students need to know that when teachers grade their work, the process is not based upon who they are as people. Instead, they see clear evidence that the teacher is looking solely at what they have learned in connection with a specific goal. To make sure they receive that message loud and clear, Table 4.1 points out that the language we use when developing criteria for success must be kid-friendly. Unlike some of the methods teachers apply to assess students, particularly in the data analysis realm, criteria for success are what is known as "student-facing," which means that kids are the primary audience for understanding the criteria. Think about the process of feedback from a logical perspective: If students do not fully understand the expectations teachers set, how can they meet them?

It would be remiss to address effective feedback without also considering the role of timeliness in how students receive what teachers have to say about their work. Depending on the type of task students engage in, the immediacy of how teachers respond might be more or less productive. As researchers Bryan Goodwin and Kristen Miller write:

> When students are acquiring new, complex knowledge or skills, real-time checks for understanding and tips can prevent them from developing misconceptions or incorrect practices. But when they are extending and applying knowledge (for example, writing an essay or solving a complex theorem), delaying feedback somewhat can enable them to self-correct, develop perseverance, and take responsibility for their own learning objectives. (2012)

The ideal balance of when to give students feedback can be difficult to determine, but as Goodwin and Miller point out, the type of cognitive task in which students engage should provide guidance about how quickly to react. When the goal is to build critical thinking capacity, for example, jumping in with immediate feedback (especially a verbal response) can limit student capacity. However, when kids stand on more uncertain ground with newer content, it can be reassuring to have a timelier response that indicates whether they understand the material.

It is impossible to help students see their academic identities in a more flattering light if they are never able to understand how to take control of their growth. When success is perceived as arbitrary, or personal, or opaque, or a game of luck, the result is learned helplessness and a sense of internal ineptitude that follows students past their years of schooling and into adulthood. On the other hand, if we pinpoint exactly how students can show their success, both teachers and students will benefit from a higher sense of visibility toward shared learning targets.

Feedback on Feedback

In a meeting to plan an upcoming professional development training for teachers, I once made the mistake of suggesting to a school-based team that we skip the usual close-of-session survey in favor of a different method to gather voice data.

"The problem with surveys," I explained, "is that the results rarely make it back to participants. That's why a relatively low percentage of attendees tend to fill out surveys to begin with. They don't see what benefits exist for them, and we forget to close the loop of communicating what we did with the data."

The remainder of the meeting was a little frustrating. Somehow, the narrative of "Miriam hates surveys" took hold as a joke that came up repeatedly, and while I love a good laugh, the inaccuracy of that statement grated on my nerves. Truth be told, I hold great appreciation for surveys when those who administer them execute the process properly, analyze the results thoughtfully, and (here's the sticking point) follow through on adjustments or actions in a way that is visible and transparent to all. Otherwise, similar to the "feedback hole" described at the start of this chapter, a "survey hole" threatens to swallow participant feedback into an abyss that will never see the light of day.

Most adults have experienced this feeling, so it does not take much imagination to understand where students are coming from when they feel that providing their opinions is either futile or unsafe. With the former, filling out a survey for the sake of filling it out is checking a box and does not drive any real change. In such cases, prior experience has demonstrated that whoever provides this survey does nothing with the results—or at least, nothing that respondents can clearly see. With the latter, a far more unstable situation exists in which the survey acts as a "gotcha" to ferret out undesirable opinions and call those who express them to the carpet.

Needless to say, while both of these situations abuse the true purpose of getting feedback, the second situation indicates a far more dysfunctional (and harmful) work or classroom environment. Adults might be able to transfer to new workplaces, but students do not have that option.

Assuming everyone understands the importance of gathering and acting upon student voice, moving forward with a process that includes what is known as a "feedback on feedback" structure is vitally important to building classrooms that value academic identity. For students to believe that teachers not only read their feedback, but also make changes to the way class functions based upon what they suggest, a process must be put in place that makes time for teachers to share the results of voice data. For example, if I give students a quick exit ticket to ask what worked for their learning today and what did not, the best way to respond to this information is to address it as soon as possible by sharing what will happen as next steps, ideally the next time class meets.

In action, providing feedback on feedback is stunningly straightforward. With the exit ticket question shared above, suppose several students have shared that a group discussion worked best for their learning, but that it was hard to sit still for so long. The next day, the teacher can incorporate the impact of what everyone shared as part of framing the day's learning by saying something like, "Your exit ticket responses yesterday indicated that you liked all the discussion, but that you wanted more movement. So, today we will be standing up a lot more to work with partners across the room." With this simple addition to the start of the class and a very slight adjustment on the part of the teacher for the day's instruction, students will see plainly that the act of valuing their feedback is not all talk—it literally results in action. From the teacher's perspective, the lesson plan itself does not change, nor does the content; rather, the method of how students achieve their partner discussion undergoes a slight alteration.

The trust that comes from incorporating a feedback-on-feedback structure as part of regular instruction cannot be underestimated. As education professors and researchers John Hattie and Helen Timperley (2007) assert, "feedback has no effect in a vacuum; to be powerful in its effect, there must be a learning context to which feedback is addressed" (p. 82). If I make a general comment to my entire class that the central arguments in their writing are too vague, my ideas might not be understood or well received. On the other hand, if I hand back essays and share that everyone struggled with clear thesis statements, and then we workshop a better way to write them on the spot, students will have the necessary information about how to improve with a process that makes my thoughts about their improvement more immediate and visible. Along the same lines, if I wait to address the voice feedback students provide for several days or weeks, they will not necessarily remember what was going on when they shared their thoughts, and the effectiveness of the process in the context of learning will be compromised.

To avoid pitfalls that can result from ineffectively implementing a feedback-on-feedback framing piece for instruction, Table 4.2 provides some ideal practices in contrast with less productive methods.

TABLE 4.2

Do This	Not That
Gather some form of voice data regularly to test the temperature of the classroom.	Intuit or assume what students may be feeling or experiencing.
Address any feedback on feedback in the subsequent class period.	Wait to share the results of student feedback until a more convenient time.
Tell students in specific terms what changes will result from their feedback.	Indicate that there will be changes, but be vague about what they look like.
Address openly which suggestions cannot be carried out, and why that is.	Address that some changes cannot be adopted, but do not explain why.
Check in after implementing a suggestion to see how students received the change.	Assume that any action taken as the result of feedback was well received.

Two consistent patterns emerge within Table 4.2: transparency and action. Over time, as students see the consistent application of their ideas to instruction accompanied with an open conversation about how their feedback adds value to the classroom community, the results are formidable. Not only does mutual trust flourish, but students also see the importance of shared accountability for learning, which further adds to their overarching sense of academic identity.

What can teachers do when feedback is not actionable for any reason, whether the suggestions students make are unreasonable or simply not possible based upon curriculum goals or other constraints? In keeping with the safe spaces we seek to establish and maintain, the decisions teachers make about what we don't do must also be shared with students openly, whether that happens in front of an entire class or with individuals in private conversation. Just because an idea does not work does not make the person who made the suggestion illegitimate or unintelligent—in fact, quite the opposite. The most divergent or risky thinkers might not always see a widespread acceptance of their thoughts, but teachers can validate creative approaches by celebrating feedback on feedback for the way it brings all students more actively into being part of a collaborative learning experience.

Most of us have been brought up to embrace the ideas we agree with, or that most align with the way we like to operate. This limited way of looking at the world around us may be comforting, but it hardly encourages the growth of those who have an entirely different way of seeing things. When teachers frame classes consistently by sharing and acting upon student feedback, we open the door to perspectives and ideas that increase the capacity of everyone in the classroom.

From Feedback to Trust

One sunny spring day, Julie walks into her U.S. history class and dumps her things on a chair before walking up to the board. She is a little nearsighted but keeps resisting wearing the glasses buried deep in her backpack, so her custom is to examine the agenda on the smartboard up close before the period begins.

At the top of the agenda, she sees an item that excites her: "Build Your Own *Jeopardy!*"

I wonder if that's what I suggested, she thinks. *Where's Ms. Helm?*

"Hey," a voice says behind Julie, "isn't that what you asked for last week?"

Julie turns around and sees one of her favorite classmates, Kyle, putting his backpack onto his own chair. "Yep," she says. "I hope so, anyway."

Over the next few minutes, students drift in and Julie resists the urge to bother Ms. Helm in the hallway. She knows that her teacher likes to stand outside the room and greet people, chatting with them about inconsequential things until the bell rings.

When class begins, Ms. Helm gets everybody's attention. "Last week, you may remember that I asked for some feedback about how you all would like to review for our upcoming test. We had a couple of suggestions that involved playing some games, and one of them had an interesting twist. Instead of me coming up with the questions, the idea was to have groups develop questions in advance and use them to play *Jeopardy!*"

As soon as Ms. Helm names the game, there is a stirring of excitement and she laughs. "I know, I know. Who doesn't love *Jeopardy!*, right? We always get a little nutty with it. But before anyone starts to get that side of themselves going, I want to highlight the first step. The game itself will be tomorrow, and per the agenda, we're building the questions today."

"Will we play any of the other games that people asked for?" Kyle asks.

"Good question," Ms. Helm says. "My goal is that at some point, we will get to all of the suggestions that make sense for what we are learning, but it might not be for this unit. Also, if we can't get to all of them, I want you to know that it's because I couldn't find a way to make the game fit with the concepts we're learning about. Let me show you something."

Turning to the smartboard, Ms. Helm taps the large screen to bring up the next slide. It is divided into two parts: one is titled "suggestions" and the second is "actions."

"Up here, we have the ideas you suggested regarding test review, and here is what we'll be doing over the next few weeks as a result. For example, you'll see that some learners asked for a quiet period to study in class, so that is going to happen later this week. And another student wanted the class to generate a review sheet together, which I'm hoping we can blend with our *Jeopardy!* activity today to make both things happen."

She gives the class a moment to read the slide before moving ahead to the next one. "You have this in our online classroom to look at, but I wanted to take a moment to address the feedback that is harder for me to accommodate. For example, one student asked about taking an open-note test, and while I appreciate that suggestion, it's not one I can accommodate right now. You see, the curriculum we use specifically indicates that students will demonstrate their understanding with a variety of skills, and one of those includes applying what we learn in a writing prompt on assessments without the aid of any materials."

"Bummer," a voice from somewhere in the middle of the class intones, and everyone laughs.

"Hey, can't blame anyone for trying," Ms. Helm says. "And this other idea I can't accommodate is about digging deeper into a specific website that analyzes the results of presidential elections on a global scale. Unfortunately, this resource is not approved by our school district, so we can't use it. But I always appreciate it when you all look for new ways to access ideas, so keep at it."

"Seems like there should be lots of sites we can look at for that," a girl near the front suggests. "And a few of those have to be approved, right?"

"One would hope," Ms. Helm agrees. "And I encourage you to look. But for now, we can turn our focus to creating some *Jeopardy!* questions for tomorrow. Does that sound good?"

The students in Ms. Helm's class have the advantage of working with a teacher who takes the time to build trust through feedback. When students have evidence that teachers are listening, the process of building trust becomes quicker and more meaningful. If we were to gather some qualitative data to determine the benefit of Ms. Helm's approach, it would look something like Table 4.3, which tracks the feedback-on-feedback process in light of what action was taken, as well as what could not be implemented and why.

TABLE 4.3

You Said	We Did	We Did Not, Because
Can we play more games for test review?	This week, we will develop questions for *Jeopardy!* and play.	While we can do this more, it will not always work based on what might be happening.
I found a great website to analyze presidential elections globally. Can we use it?	Can the class look for other approved sites that contain similar content?	I took a look, and the site is unfortunately not approved for school use.

Think about the power of sharing a chart like the one featured in Table 4.3 with students, especially in a place where everyone can access the information, like an online classroom portal. Gathering student voice for framing the learning is highly effective, but posting it as a type of running record is an even more significant way to show students over time that their comments and ideas have an enormous impact on the class.

When teachers seek to build trust with students, the process has to be more profound than showing up, being approachable, and designing engaging instruction. Students need to know that their work is considered worthy, whether that takes the form of frequent and timely feedback on assignments or through listening to ideas and acting upon them visibly. Only then can genuine trust, which is earned rather than bestowed, continue to build with each passing day of instruction.

Feedback Tools

"I got a C," Mara says to her friend, Priya. "What did you get?"

Priya frowns at the rubric that is stapled to the back of her paper. "I got a B," she says. "But I can't read whatever Mrs. Davis put on the bottom of this. She circled a lot of fours, and that's all I see."

"I have threes," Mara says, looking at her own rubric. "And she wrote on the bottom, 'Needs more analysis.' I'm not sure what that means."

Priya points to a list next to the numbers. "It looks like she categorized everything based on different writing skills. Like, this column is for mechanics, and this one is for being on topic. But I don't know how your comment relates to that. You could ask her."

"Maybe," Mara responds. She glances toward Mrs. Davis, who is frowning as she writes out a bathroom pass at her desk. "Then again, maybe not."

When teachers hand back assignments with an attached rubric, the mistaken assumption is that students will understand how they have been assessed. More often than not, unfortunately, the rubric enters the grading process too late. To compound confusion, rubrics are also written to be teacher-facing, which means that while adults perfectly understand a lot of the edujargon, kids either expend a great deal of effort to translate what terms mean, or more often, they give up entirely and relegate rubrics to a circular file, aka the trash can.

If teachers want students to understand what feedback means, as well as how they are assessed, the tools we use must be specifically designed for understanding. Thinking about the technical aspects of a rubric, the highest point of performance (usually also the highest number students can attain on any given assignment) is also the criteria for success. When we communicate these criteria at the same time that students receive an assignment, and ensure they understand the expectations for how they meet criteria, their eventual success is far more assured.

To that end, the criteria for the success grid featured in Table 4.4 provides a visual method for helping students understand what they need to do when completing a writing task.

TABLE 4.4

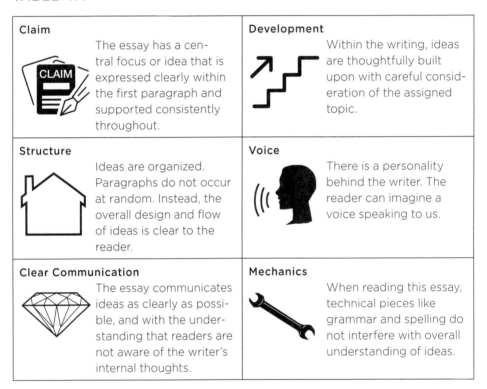

Claim	Development
The essay has a central focus or idea that is expressed clearly within the first paragraph and supported consistently throughout.	Within the writing, ideas are thoughtfully built upon with careful consideration of the assigned topic.
Structure	**Voice**
Ideas are organized. Paragraphs do not occur at random. Instead, the overall design and flow of ideas is clear to the reader.	There is a personality behind the writer. The reader can imagine a voice speaking to us.
Clear Communication	**Mechanics**
The essay communicates ideas as clearly as possible, and with the understanding that readers are not aware of the writer's internal thoughts.	When reading this essay, technical pieces like grammar and spelling do not interfere with overall understanding of ideas.

In Table 4.4, the traditional "six traits" of a writing rubric has been shifted so that the intended audience can more fully comprehend what is required of them. Students might not be able to parse out the jargon of more traditional rubrics, but this visual, user-friendly grid presents a far more appealing approach. As students review their own work or engage in a peer editing process, they look at one another's grids and annotate them for what still needs to be improved. The teacher can use the same tool when handing final products back to students, and then everyone will be more familiar with how this visual take on assessment works to identify where writing stands in relation to an identified goal.

Making the process of being successful transparent so that students see themselves in a more positive light from an academic perspective is just one action teachers can take to make the process of writing instruction reach kids in a profound way that impacts their identity. In addition, considering how to communicate with students so that teachers can adjust language to match their needs is imperative if learning targets are to become more visible.

To bridge a frequent divide in clarity between teachers and students, the language of feedback chart in Table 4.5 offers some alternatives to more common phrases that teachers use around children that might be misunderstood , that represent a fixed mindset, or that are overly opaque. By consciously shifting how teachers talk to kids when providing feedback, mutual understanding becomes an even more attainable goal.

TABLE 4.5

Instead of This . . .	Try This!
Good job!	The example in your second paragraph really helps support the overall idea beautifully.
See me.	Can we discuss the length of this essay in relation to the assignment directions?
These ideas are vague.	In your body paragraphs, elaborate ideas with detail to explain examples.
Grade: C	While this paper does not yet meet all criteria, I've marked areas for improvement.
Plot summary!	Write about how the plot helps to support your central ideas on sexism.
Please revise.	Much of this paper meets criteria, but I've highlighted areas that could use some revision.

Using language that is student-friendly cannot be underestimated in any teacher's journey to build more trust through feedback. By consciously changing the way we talk to students with phrases like the ones exemplified in Table 4.5, students will understand exactly what it takes for them to be successful in class.

Strengthening academic identity in students has so much to do with their sense of belonging in any scholarly environment. For too many kids, their confidence is curtailed when they repeatedly misunderstand the root causes that explain poor class performance. It is too easy to blame internal factors such as their own perceived lack of intelligence, or external forces like teacher favoritism or bad luck. When feedback is specific and student-friendly with clear criteria for success, not only do students have a better idea of how to do well in their classes; they also understand that academic worth is measured not by chance but by the effort they put into meeting the expectations set forth for their achievement. With that knowledge and the trust in their teachers to help them reach goals, students get that much closer to seeing themselves as worthy contributors to any classroom.

Let's think back to Dr. Benson's class at the start of this chapter. His student, Will, sits in class puzzling over what it means to have a "holistic" grade, and ultimately, he gives up trying to find out.

Now, imagine a different outcome to this scenario. Instead of handing back his holistic rubric, Dr. Benson says, "I've used our criteria for success checklist to indicate where everyone met the standard for success, and what still needs to be done. If you look at your feedback, it should help you figure out what to do next."

When Will gets his paper, he sees this:

- ~~Clear central claim~~
- One personal experience shared in the introduction
  - *The example is from the news, not personal.*
- At least three references, correctly cited
  - *I see two, not three. Let me know if that's not correct.*
- ~~Document is spell checked~~
- ~~Concluding sentence to bring ideas together~~

Will, let me know if you want to fix the items that are not crossed off as complete. Happy to help clarify anything as well. Thanks! –Dr. B.

Okay, Will thinks. *I can fix this easily enough.* He remembers being over-whelmed when he wrote this assignment, and he made some careless omissions. He'll send Dr. Benson an email to let him know he plans to revise his work.

Changing the way we give feedback might require a little bit of adjustment, but no seismic shifts are necessary. Once students understand the value of the process, their investment saves everyone from experiencing a vicious cycle of angst. Instead, teachers and students share in a classroom in which academic identity can be celebrated transparently and openly.

Cross-Content Strategy

Math, Middle School
Contributors: BensonVoss (coteaching team)

Context:
BensonVoss is a coteaching team made up of Amber Benson and Ruby Voss. They have been together for five and a half years and were recently awarded the honor of 2022 AMLE National Educator of the Year.

Strategy: Data Analytics in Room E12
BensonVoss data meetings are a strategy used to build students' self-confidence as they grow to see themselves as *data analysts*. Students are stakeholders in their education, and this process affirms that belief. They use graphs developed from the prior week's assessment to determine which Math 8 standards they have achieved, which they are close to but have not achieved just yet, and which will require reteaching and practice. The insight that students develop and articulate as they watch their class averages ebb and flow is nothing short of inspiring. Data is information, and information is power. Often, the students in classes featured below (60% of whom have IEP, 504, and/or EL plans) have never felt powerful in math class, but class data meetings turn the tide.

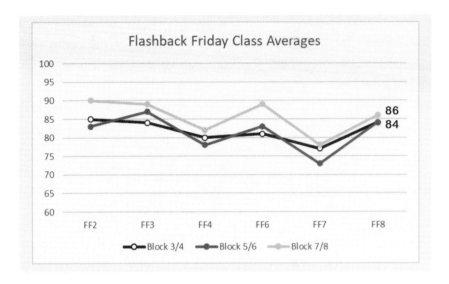

Students learn to analyze line graphs and discuss whether their class improved or not. They also discuss the slope of the lines to determine rates of increases and decreases in class averages. The three classes choose their own creative names, like "Shrek" and "SpongeBob." The "Oreo Lovers'" class data is shown in more detail below.

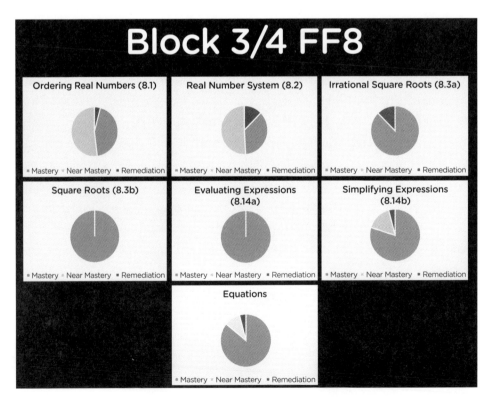

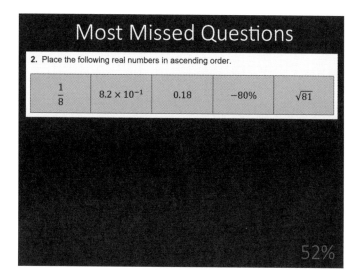

Students discuss their class performance on Math 8 Standards and determine which skills will be spiraled into the week's Focus activities and the week's assessment. As an option, the BensonVoss teaching team sometimes offers looking at just a portion of a skill to check students' understanding rather than having them complete an entire problem.

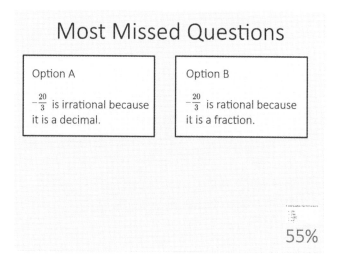

Students practice the most missed questions and discuss common misconceptions and errors to better understand where mistakes may have occurred and how to correct those mistakes. Once again, this process normalizes and celebrates how errors lead to learning and growth.

CHAPTER 5

The Space Between: Navigating Personal and Academic Identity

Making Space

James has nowhere to go at lunchtime. The high school cafeteria is rowdy and overcrowded. The hallways are lined with kids chatting noisily or streaming content incessantly on their phones, and it's too cold to eat outside on the track, which is his go-to spot in decent weather.

It's not that nobody likes James, or that he doesn't feel vaguely friendly toward some of his classmates, depending on the situation. He thinks that people probably perceive him as being shy, and that's true. He likes school for what he learns, and he doesn't enjoy socializing much with peers. He knows that is not the way most people work, but he is comfortable with his own preferences.

As James wanders down the hall looking for a place to eat, he sees Ms. Saunders coming toward him. She teaches his American history class, and he likes her. She is always friendly, but also seems to sense that he is never in the mood for too much small talk. Instead, she keeps their conversations in class focused on the material so that he doesn't feel uncomfortable.

"James!" Ms. Saunders smiles at him, pausing amid her brisk steps. "What are you up to? Did you eat already?"

"Not yet," James says, trying but not quite succeeding at making eye contact with her.

Ms. Saunders has been teaching James all year, and has also been observing his behavior both in and out of class. She likes to take walks outside the building on her lunch break and often notices him sitting alone on the bleachers by the track, eating out of an insulated lunch bag with a book open in his lap. While James is excessively shy, Ms. Saunders finds him to be a very sweet kid who cares deeply about learning. Trying to figure out where he could eat, her brain goes to the group that plays board games in a classroom at lunch with a well-liked colleague in her department, and she quickly dismisses that idea. Some kids might like that setting, but it doesn't work for every kid, and certainly not for James.

Suddenly, inspiration strikes. "I have an idea," she says. "Come with me."

With some degree of hesitation, James follows Ms. Saunders down the hall until they reach the school media center. She guides him through the main area filled with books and computers until they reach a side room toward the back. In the middle is a large table where two students are sitting. One is working on a handout while the other is reading a textbook. On the side of the room is a refrigerator and sink, along with a few comfortable chairs, one of them occupied by a teacher who is tapping away on a laptop.

James feels like he is trespassing. "Isn't this the homework help room?"

"Technically, yes," she admits. "But what if I get special permission for you to eat back here, as long as you either read your book or work on something for class? I can even meet you here once or twice a week to see what you're doing for our class if you'd like."

"Are you sure?" James asks. It seems too good to be true to have a quiet indoor space where nobody will bother him.

Ms. Saunders nods. "Of course. This room is always available through a signup sheet online, and I'll just sign you up each week until you'd like to try something else. And you don't have to come every day, either. I'll tell the media specialist it's your call."

As he looks around, James doesn't know what to say to express his gratitude. He has always liked Ms. Saunders, but it seems as though she understands him more than he gave her credit for. Barely audible, he says, "Thank you."

"Oh, please don't thank me," Ms. Saunders says. "It's no problem. I'm always happy to help anyone who cares as much as you do about school. How about you get settled in? I'm going to get you signed up now."

With one last wave, she leaves the room and James takes a seat at the large table, pulling out his lunch bag and his book. For so many years, he has felt as though nobody sees him. It feels great to know that at least one person in this building might appreciate what he has to offer, even if he acts differently than most kids his age. With sudden energy, James reaches back into his bag and takes out his American history assignment. It is certainly good enough to be turned in, but now, he wants to take another look. Ms. Saunders deserves his best work.

From "Otherness" to Belonging

Though he struggles socially, a student like James in the scenario above is lucky in one respect: He feels a sense of belonging in academic settings. In some ways, school is a safe space for him as he engages with course content. In other ways, he feels what is known as "otherness" during unstructured time in the day when most kids frequently seek the refuge of one another's company.

Teachers face the complex instructional challenge of navigating the space between reaching out to students on a personal level and remaining grounded in building academic belonging for all kids by maintaining a strong connection between course content and identity. While many students veer in the opposite direction of James by opting to socialize as much as possible, the goal for teachers is to strike a balance in how classes are set up so that we do not accidentally cross lines that lean too heavily toward getting too personal or too businesslike. With the former, adults are overly familiar with students, and the latter approach is perceived as cold or heartless.

Think about the presuppositions that students bring into classrooms before they even meet their teachers. For example, I spent the majority of my own adolescent years assuming that math class just wasn't for me, a belief that was as faulty as it was damaging. Somewhere in my childhood, a family member affirmed this belief with a careless comment: "It's okay that you don't do well in math. I never did, either." Luckily, I developed a mindset in early adulthood that helped me see that I did well in math when I made the effort to achieve, but many people never have the same epiphany. Furthermore, for teachers who work with secondary-age learners, many students have not yet learned to question some of the more damaging assumptions that have been built up over time about what they can and cannot do. Social psychologist Paul O'Keefe et al. (2021) addresses the unfortunate influence that deficit perspective has on student behavior:

> Students with a fixed mindset of interest tend to view interests as inherent and relatively unchangeable. From this perspective, once a student feels they have "found" their interests, they have no reason to explore new or different academic areas. Therefore, a student with interests solely in the arts, for example, might not deeply engage in their math or science courses. By contrast, those with a growth mindset of interest view interests as cultivated and developable. Therefore, even if they already hold strong interests in one area, they might could [sic] still explore other areas. Such a student would be more likely to engage in their math and science courses and, as a result, become more interested in the topics and learn more. (para. 11)

Helping students see another perspective through questioning the ideas they have held to be correct about themselves for so long must therefore be a conscious exercise. By providing an accessible entry point to think about how everyone reacts to tasks they perceive as being too challenging, the reflective activity in Box 5.1 helps both kids and adults alike consider the way they limit their own experiences.

BOX 5.1

Personal Reflection

DIRECTIONS:

Think of a time when you were younger and began to believe that something was too hard for you. It could be school-related or personal.

Brainstorm thoughts about what happened, using the questions below as a guide to your thoughts.

- What triggered your thinking about the challenge of the task? What exactly happened? Who said what?
- What were your feelings at first? How did they change as time passed?
- Were there consequences that had an impact on the future because of your thinking that way?
- How might you confront and question the beliefs you have about your ability with this challenge?

Reflect upon your thoughts above in connection with other challenges you face.

Is your inner voice correct about what you can or cannot do? If so, why? If not, what can you do to change the way you see your own abilities? Finally, what actions might be needed to try a new approach?

Without explicitly facing perceived barriers to success to begin the process of dismantling them, people of all ages run the risk of spending the entirety of their schooling (not to mention the years beyond) believing that they are incapable of being successful with certain tasks or endeavors. With that, they will remain in a space of "otherness," remaining firmly convinced that certain avenues are forever closed to them.

As teachers, it is our job to help students achieve a sense of belonging in school without going too far into their personal territory. With activities like the one featured in Box 5.1, a major question teachers might face is how to help students process the information that they uncover about themselves and what they have presumed to be too difficult. In a safe, well-developed classroom community that has already progressed through much of the year, students might be able to share some of their experiences with one another. Toward the earlier portion of the year or in a less secure environment, the reflections that result from Box 5.1 are best left to the individual to process alone or perhaps in a written response for the teacher's eyes only.

In the continuing quest to help students discover more about themselves and their place in the world, a self-exploration like the one in Box 5.2 is a creative way to approach learning about academic identity. Perhaps several times in their school careers, students are asked to describe physical attributes of people, experiences, and/or places. By focusing on nonphysical attributes only, the journey toward discovering the scholarly self grows a little clearer.

BOX 5.2

Self-Description

DIRECTIONS:

In your journal, write a description of yourself using the following guidelines.

- Focus most of all on your inner self—your personality, your likes and dislikes, and all other elements that make you . . . well, you.
- Avoid using physical descriptors, especially obvious ones like "straight brown hair" or similar.
- The description can stand on its own or be taken from a situation or scenario to represent a moment in time from your life.
- While this description digs deep, do not reveal anything that might be overly private or that would be best kept confidential.
- The tone of this is up to you. You can be serious, funny, or anywhere in between. You may also write from any perspective you choose.
- Use this as an opportunity for self-appreciation, and to showcase what you most like about yourself.

While students may have spent a lot of time (particularly in writing descriptive pieces) focusing on how things appear, the inward look that Box 5.2 requires journeys far more deeply into what it means to have worth in the world around us, and what larger goals or dreams exist beyond what is visible.

The realization that everyone has a contribution to make is so import-ant for students to experience, especially when their talents might not be as clearly on display in a school setting. I well remember the rare oppor-tunities I had in middle school to showcase my love of the performing arts, and my teachers would often react to the difference between my shy classroom demeanor and a bolder persona in theater with observa-tions like, "I didn't know you had it in you." I was lucky enough to have at least this chance to display a side of myself within a school building that was typically unseen, but think about students who never have the same experience. What if their talents go entirely unrecognized anywhere in school? In that event, their sense of belonging will continue to plummet as they conclude their strengths are unimportant.

When there is no clear pathway for students with a wide array of skills to demonstrate their value, teachers must provide the opportunity for them to do so. The activities in Tables 5.1 and 5.2 pave the way for stu-dent thinking around challenging damaging misconceptions about what is too hard, and for considering what everyone has to offer to the spaces around them both from an academic and a personal perspective. Then, once students begin to explore their own belonging and move away from "otherness," our job is to judiciously help them discover their sense of place and efficacy by walking a careful line between building academic identity without moving into territory that is too personal or traumatic.

Where is the Line? Setting Boundaries

The early years of teaching may be marked with cringe-worthy moments and more mistakes than anyone would like, but no matter how many years a teacher has been in the classroom, falling down is a part of the job that should be embraced for the growth it engenders. Still, that doesn't prevent anyone from feeling bad about errors of judgment or mishaps that occur.

In the first few years of my career, I distributed a popular memoir for text study that produced a high level of interest from twelfth-grade stu-dents. Even better, the book seemed to speak with the most resonance to students who were usually less avid readers, and I saw more engagement from them during this unit than any other. When the class finished read-ing the book, I liked to show the film version as a reward of sorts, and conversations about the differences between book and film were enthusiastic. "The book is so much better," kids would say, and I felt that happy English teacher glow at their appreciation for literacy over screen time.

One year, I happened to be looking at students while they were watching the movie, and one boy had an expression on his face that made my heart run cold. He was clearly in pain, and the source of his angst appeared to be emotional, likely emanating from what was onscreen. I turned to see what was happening in the scene and saw that the main character's abusive stepfather was hitting him. In a moment, I realized that this student could be reliving his own traumatic experiences, and I had made a serious misjudgment in showing this scene to the class. At the time, I had to handle the situation reactively with the help of a school counselor, but I learned a lot in the coming years about staying mindful of boundaries that may emerge more subtly, but that are no less important to maintain so that students trust teachers enough to learn with them.

Furthermore, however willing students may be to work cooperatively with teachers, having additional stressors that creep into a classroom environment can result in lower achievement. As researchers and education experts Laura Hernandez and Linda Darling-Hammond (2022) state:

> Neuroscience and research on learning make it clear that social, emotional, and cognitive experiences are intertwined and influence how we learn. Having trusting relationships and experiencing positive emotions, such as interest and excitement, open the mind to learning. Negative emotions, such as anxiety or self-doubt, reduce the brain's capacity to learn when left unmitigated. (para. 1)

Clearly, even when kids give their best efforts to the work they do and value their learning process, having experiences in class that are damaging can make all the difference between being successful in a trusting classroom space that encourages the healthy development of academic identity as opposed to creating a situation that shuts students down, intentionally or not.

In the quest to form relationships with students that help them achieve a stronger sense of academic identity, teachers may be overly wary of being either too personal or too distant. Box 5.3 presents some strategies for checking in with our own behavior toward students, not just in terms of ensuring that we remain mindful of how we interact with each individual, but also in achieving a better balance that allows for more meaningful connections.

BOX 5.3

Self-Check: Balancing Relationships

KNEE-JERK RESPONSES

- When students ask questions that are tangential or not clearly related to content, do I shut the questions down quickly or take a minute to think about how to reply?
- If I have one product in mind and students ask for another option, do I consider it, or am I quick to refuse? If the latter, why do I say no?
- During class, how do I respond when students ask me personal questions? Do I automatically not answer, or do I consider the question's possible relevance to how the student is approaching the day's learning?
- How open am I to alternate points of view about class concepts and topics, particularly more open-ended or subjective ideas?

METHOD OF QUESTIONING

- When I am trying to learn about my students, do I ask follow-up questions if they are not responsive, or am I comfortable with not pursuing the answers?
- Are the questions I ask mainly closed questions with "yes" or "no" answers, or do I pose open-ended questions that rely more on higher-order thinking skills?
- Do my questions remain rooted only in class content, or do I form connections between what we learn and what students experience? If the former, why have I made that decision?
- In my class, are students encouraged to formulate and ask questions on a regular basis, and are they given time and space to share these questions with me and with one another? If so, what types of question protocols do I teach?

LEVEL OF CONVERSATION

- If I am in the same space with students I do not know well or feel comfortable with, is the room silent?
- Is discourse encouraged in my class, or do I consider a quiet room to be a better-managed learning environment? In either case, why do I feel this way?
- Do students have ample opportunity to talk to one another about what they are learning? Roughly how much class time is allocated for students to engage in conversation?
- When students struggle to have meaningful conversations about course content, what kinds of support do I provide to help them?

AWARENESS AND FAMILIARITY

- If someone asked me to share what I know about any given student on my roster, how much information could I provide without consulting any resources?
- Do I know a disproportionate amount about some students as opposed to others? If so, why is that? If not, what are my strategies for getting to know my students?
- When I learn personal details about students, how do I use that information to help them progress academically? If that is not something I do, how could I start?
- What areas would I like to strengthen in order to connect what I know about the personal details in my students' lives to how my purposeful awareness helps them achieve more?

It might be impossible for any teacher to strike the perfect balance of connecting to students personally while still maximizing their academic growth, but the questions that Box 5.3 poses move us closer to a level of awareness about strengths and areas for improvement in our own relationships with each member of the class.

Teachers who push back on making more purposeful connections with students that navigate a fine line between personal and academic interests will rightly point out that boundaries, already complicated to identify, rarely represent a fixed point. As what constitutes "too far" may shift around teachers with each individual encounter, it is sometimes harder to avoid territory that reaches the point of trauma, which students can mask in the form of behavior that is disruptive or withdrawn behavior. As education researcher and equity-informed trauma expert Alex Shevrin Venet (2018) writes: "With so much pain in the classroom, educators should be mindful that traumatic life experiences can sometimes emerge as behaviors that we might otherwise label as challenging." To that point, when students act out in classes and teachers worry about crossing into harmful territory with how to address behavior, it is always important to lean on the experts within the building, most notably school counselors.

When that social–emotional expertise is not necessary for instruction to progress, what can teachers do to establish and maintain their awareness of social–emotional needs? According to Shevrin Venet, who has gathered data around the most advisable approaches to incorporating an SEL lens into classroom spaces, it helps when teachers recognize that "the social and emotional work has to start with themselves. Educators who see the value of a practice in their own lives are more likely to be passionate advocates, and the learning ecosystem is only truly healthy when all members of the community are thriving." True, teachers are human and may, therefore, not be able to prevent every misstep or avoid making mistakes in relating to students, but being an advocate for mindfulness around emotional wellness is a good place to start.

Going back to my own mistakes, when I showed the movie clip to my class and inadvertently hurt a student in the process, I learned a hard lesson. Sometimes, we inadvertently cause damage by miscalculating where the line is that cannot be crossed. However, the beauty of teaching is that mistakes, no matter how painful, have a clear purpose in preventing people from erring the same way again. Even better, everyone can grow a little more each day by taking what works, building upon it, and fixing what does not work with added insight about how to move forward in the quest to build student confidence in their own ability.

The Right Connections

Victor reaches the door of his classroom and is confronted by a sign: "Period 3 is meeting in the library today."

Uh-oh, Victor thinks. *Hope it's not another project.*

Luckily, his third period class isn't far from the library, so he manages to get to his destination and snag a seat at one of the coveted bean bag chairs before the bell rings. When his teacher sees Victor, he just smiles and shakes his head. "Don't worry, Victor," Mr. Drake says. "I won't make you move."

The class starts and Victor learns that everyone is in the library to select a nonfiction book. "Any book is fine that is in this section," Mr. Drake says, pointing at one set of shelves.

"There should be plenty of choices. You'll be reading this book along with other shorter pieces I assign, and then you'll write a nonfiction piece of your own that borrows one element from your book, whether it relates to topic or author style. There are lots of ways you could go about it."

After going over the assignment sheet in some more detail, Mr. Drake lets everyone have 15 minutes to browse the shelves and select a book. It's crowded, so Victor hangs back for a couple of minutes. Seeing him on his chair, Mr. Drake walks over. He is holding a book in his hands and gives it to Victor.

"What's this?" Victor asks, looking at the book. It's called *Born a Crime*, and he sees the author is Trevor Noah.

"I know how much you like *The Daily Show*, so I figured you might be interested in this book he wrote," Mr. Drake explains.

Victor doesn't want to be rude, but he also thinks about being stuck with a book for a few weeks that he didn't pick and decides to speak his mind. "That's really nice of you, but I mainly talk about the show because it connects to a lot of our discussions about current events. I have a lot of other interests."

"Oh, my bad," Mr. Drake says. "I didn't realize. No worries."

"I mean, I appreciate it," Victor says, working hard to be diplomatic. "But there's a lot you don't know about me. You know, stuff that doesn't happen in our class."

"Right," Mr. Drake says. "Like your fascination with making gigantic Play Doh sculptures." He smiles to show that he is joking.

"Ha, right," Victor says. "Actually, that sounds like a cool hobby. I kind of wish I did that."

"Me too," Mr. Drake confides. "Now, are you ready to head over there and select something that you're actually interested in reading?"

"Yep," Victor says. "And I'll put this one back on the shelf to save you a trip. Thanks."

As he watches Victor head toward the stacks, Mr. Drake turns over a phrase a few times in his head that Victor just spoke: "There's a lot you don't know about me."

It's true enough, Mr. Drake reflects. *But a project like this will help me learn more about him.*

With a foundation for a trusting relationship already in evidence between Victor and Mr. Drake, a misunderstanding about what book Victor would like to read results in a frank conversation with an ideal outcome. But what happens when the connections we build with students do not have that same firm grounding? Sometimes, students and teachers get off to a rocky start with one another. The good news is the issue can usually be repaired by removing obstacles to meaningful interactions with students and by connecting to them more profoundly.

The key to creating a stronger relationship that moves beyond rapport lies in how teachers design instruction, as well as how we communicate with students about how they are progressing. It is not enough to hope that kids understand the likelihood of good intentions; they must also be explicitly informed about what happens behind the scenes when teachers create assignments that are built to determine what students know and what gaps may still exist.

In Box 5.4, students experience an accessible, thought-provoking representation of how subjects with content standards that are perceived as subjective might be approached from the perspective of the way teachers develop concrete criteria for success.

BOX 5.4

The Perfect Apple

How do we look at subjective things objectively? Is that possible? We're about to find out!

In your table groups, you will see a plate of apple slices. Please wait to eat them until the directions ask you to do so!

STEP ONE:

Think about what a perfect apple is like. What criteria does it have to meet to be considered ideal to eat? Discuss for a few minutes.

STEP TWO:

In your table groups, develop a list of at least five criteria that an apple should meet using the attached handout.

Example: The perfect apple must be crunchy and crisp, not mushy.

STEP THREE:

Eat one of the apple slices and rate it on a scale of 1 to 5 (with 5 being the best) based on how well the apple meets the criteria your group developed.

Note: you must use the criteria to do this, not your instinct or gut feelings!

REFLECT:

1. What did you notice about the process of creating joint criteria with others?
2. How was the activity challenging? What worked, and what didn't?
3. Did your expectations for the result of the apple rating match the criteria you set? Why or why not?
4. What does this activity potentially demonstrate about how assignments that seem to be subjective are graded?
5. How is this activity not representative of the grading process? Hint: Think about how your group determined the criteria for the "perfect" apple.
6. What do you wish teachers would do when they grade based on what seems like opinion rather than an objective measure?

The rationale behind Box 5.4 is not just about transparency; it is also about making sure that students do not see the assessment process as personal. True, developing criteria for a so-called "perfect" apple might be based on inclination, but skillful teachers can emphasize that this activity is not a complete parallel to the exact process of formulating assessment "look-fors," as indicated in the fifth reflection question. A substantial benefit to undergoing this exercise is that groups must come to agreement on setting norms for their apples, much like teams of teachers must agree on how to determine point values. When this activity is concluded, the cognitive empathy that kids experience further paves the way for their understanding of the most beneficial connections teachers can make beyond knowing students as individuals and truly developing their scholarly selves by completing activities that have visible, fair targets.

The importance of opening the door for increased interpersonal learning connectivity remains a priority and is most effective when any work that teachers do around rapport also has firm grounding in course content. That is why writing "games," which appear on the surface to be a silly way to blow off some steam in a specific medium, are so conducive to building academic rapport. Writing, an inherently personal endeavor, helps teachers bridge the gap between how students feel and what they create. Consider the "Five Nouns" activity featured in Box 5.5, which on the surface simply looks like a way for students to create a collaborative story.

BOX 5.5

Five Nouns

PART ONE: WRITING!

- Take the provided sheet of scratch paper and rip it into five roughly equal pieces.
- On each individual piece, write a noun. It can be any noun you like, as long as it is school appropriate. When you are finished, you should have five slips of paper, each with one noun.
- Fold your papers up so that the nouns are no longer visible. Place your folded papers into the open shoebox at the front of the classroom.

- When prompted, pick five slips of paper at random from the shoebox. If you select any of your own nouns, keep them. You get what you get!
- Using all five nouns, write a short story that weaves the words into a plot as seamlessly and subtly as possible. Your story need not be too long, or represent a completed product. You will have 20 minutes to write.

PART TWO: SHARING!

- We will use random calling to start a "popcorn" sharing protocol.
- While each classmate reads the story out loud, try to guess all five nouns by actively listening. Do not guess the nouns you wrote yourself: That's cheating! Otherwise, let's see how many we can guess together!

PART THREE: REFLECTION

- How did listening carefully for each noun influence your attention to and understanding of each story?
- Which stories resonated with you, and why?
- What did you enjoy about this activity? What was challenging?
- Please take a moment to stand up, walk around the room, and express appreciation for how a classmate used your nouns!

The "Five Nouns" activity holds distinct appeal for having what one of my students once called a "fun-ness quotient." However, there is also a more subversive quality to this process, one that allows students to create products with a certain degree of friction (in this case, tying many unruly and disconnected nouns into one coherent story) together. When classmates see the mutual struggle in the room and realize they are not alone in trying to work out how to do a story with words they might not be too excited to incorporate, the level of rapport around an academic exercise increases significantly.

To replicate the benefits of an activity like "Five Nouns" in all instruction and not just for intentional moments, Table 5.1 shares some possible moves that teachers can either make themselves or guide students to make for increasing their academic identity as an integrated component of regular teaching and learning.

TABLE 5.1

| Academic Identity Moves | |
Teachers	Students
Create regular opportunities for students to communicate about their learning in the four language domains: speaking, writing, reading, and listening.	During times that are set aside for sharing, work to develop complex questions or comments to share with fellow classmates about your learning.
Take time to weigh each student's comment or question. Do not respond too quickly or move on without verbally processing their contribution.	If the learning environment has proven itself to be a trusting one, take risks by speaking up with the knowledge that your ideas have value.
Ask for student feedback on a regular basis, and then circle back to questions or suggestions during the next class period with clarity and transparency.	When teachers ask for your opinion, provide it honestly and kindly. Be truthful, but also remember that your teacher is a person with feelings.
With class activities and procedures, try to vary methods of instructional delivery on a regular basis so that learning does not feel stagnant.	When learning starts to feel a little boring or repetitive, make productive suggestions to help your teacher develop some new ideas for the class instead of complaining.
When a student says or does something that feels hurtful, take some time to breathe and figure out what to do. Do not react immediately.	If you feel uncomfortable with your teacher, think about diplomatically letting them know how you feel. If their intentions are good, they will appreciate being told.

Making the right connections all the time might not be tenable when so many individual personalities are thrown into one room together, but teachers can continuously examine approaches to practice that hold both ourselves and our students accountable for doing the best possible job we can to know one another both as people and as members of a collaborative classroom community.

Reaching All Kids

A lot of kids are jealous of Melissa. How many other eighth-grade students are as popular, nice, *and* smart as she is?

That's the perception, anyway, and Melissa works hard to keep up appearances. She feels like two people: the image of herself that she has so carefully cultivated for her peers and teachers, and the *real* version of her, the one who goes home to an empty house and works through the afternoon and evening just to keep up with all the commitments she is unable to refuse without feeling bad about it.

Teachers love having Melissa in class. She is humble, funny, and never fails to do her work. When a child who might otherwise be ostracized does something odd, Melissa celebrates it, and others follow her example. She is wise beyond her years and so willing to help out that it's almost like having another adult in the room. Almost everyone who knows Melissa would be shocked if they knew that she often feels like the exact opposite of the image she projects. Everyone, that is, except Ms. Reese.

From the moment students walk into her classroom, Ms. Reese works hard to dig beneath the surface and look at what is not easily apparent. She focuses on ideas, being strategic about how she comments on what students share. Even when kids struggle to express themselves, Ms. Reese will respond by saying something like, "Let's unpack that thought. Can you explain a little bit more about that?" Her goal is not to hear what students think she wants to hear; her goal is to know more about how the students in front of her learn best.

With Melissa, Ms. Reese noticed something about her from the very first day of school. While she is certainly quick to support others and to offer help, Melissa likes to move focus away from herself. She raises her hand to support another person's contribution, or to expand upon a point that has already been expressed. In her writing, Melissa is thoughtful and clear, but she never fails to apologize when she turns in her work. "Sorry," she'll say. "This didn't turn out how I wanted it to." Almost without fail, whatever she hands in is exemplary and doesn't match her underestimation of its worth.

One day, Ms. Reese asks Melissa if she has time during lunch one day to help her create flyers for an upcoming "coffee house" event that the school newspaper is sponsoring. Always willing to help, Melissa is more than happy to assist.

After about fifteen minutes of discussing designs and clicking around in Canva, both Ms. Reese and Melissa agree upon the final version. As Melissa clicks images and manipulates them, Ms. Reese admires her work.

"You're very talented at so many things," she comments. "It must be hard to decide which activities to participate in sometimes."

"Not really," Melissa says. "I like trying a lot of things, but I wouldn't say that I'm that good at most of them."

"That's interesting, because my impression is quite different. You seem quite good at whatever you set your mind to doing."

Melissa pauses in her clicking and turns away from the computer to face Ms. Reese. "I've always felt connected to other people, and so maybe I'd like to do something someday that lets me focus on that, like being a child psychologist or something. But I'm just okay at sports, and my class stuff takes a lot of work. It's hard because I'm not naturally smart or anything."

Ms. Reese shakes her head. "Wait a minute. Who ever said that being what you call 'naturally smart' has to do with not working hard? It seems to me that the hardest working people are the ones who achieve, not the ones who expect everything to come to them without much effort."

"I wish that were true," Melissa says, "but I have a sister who is a lot older and she never had to do much at all. She still got straight As, plus she was a star cheerleader and had lots of friends. I've never been like that."

"Maybe you're not like your sister, but that doesn't have anything to do with how legitimate your intelligence is. Ever think about that?"

Melissa shrugs. "I guess." She seems disinclined to continue the conversation and turns back to the flyer draft on her screen. "I'd better get back to this so you can have it by the end of lunch."

Ms. Reese watches Melissa for a moment before deciding that she has done enough for one day. She has sown some important seeds, but it will take time for Melissa to understand that she doesn't have to pretend to be her sister to be valued. Slowly, over time, perhaps Ms. Reese can convince Melissa that she can be successful on her own terms.

When teachers seek to reach all students, nobody can be exempt from the way we design our classes to be inclusive. Whether children seem engaged or not, whether they do their assignments or not, whether they seem to be struggling or not, everyone deserves to be validated and seen. Table 5.2 exemplifies a practical way to approach making sure we make an effort toward understanding all of the students in front of us with a rotation check-in process.

TABLE 5.2

	Monday	Tuesday	Wednesday	Thursday	Friday
Assignments (Week A)	A–E	F–I	J–N	O–T	U–Z
Wellness (Week B)	U–Z	O–T	A–E	F–I	J–N

In the sample featured in Table 5.2, the importance of rotating students through a check-in with the teacher is not necessarily about the structure itself, but rather its existence and follow-through. This model involves a biweekly rotation, one focused on schoolwork and one on wellness. In this construct, the teacher takes a few minutes each day to check in with students in a specific alphabetical range. Many students might not need the time at all, indicating a "thumbs-up" or similar if they do not have concerns. Likewise, the teacher may use this time to approach only students who are more visibly in need of quick and targeted help. However, the idea behind such a rotation is to ensure that time is set aside to talk to individuals on a semi-regular basis beyond simply greetings or small talk.

Students like James, Victor, and Melissa fall into places that are less reflective of what is expected from students, areas that might not be readily apparent to less discerning eyes. To serve their needs, not to mention those of every student in the classroom, determining how to ground relationships in the context of learning is essential. The space between academic and social experience in a school building is complex to navigate, and it is inevitable that all teachers and students will stumble in their ongoing quest to understand one another. Ideally, however, the overtly expressed wish to keep trying and build classrooms that embrace student identity in all forms gets teachers one step closer to helping students see themselves in the best possible light.

Cross-Content Strategy

English Language Arts, Middle School

Contributor: Kristen Engle

Student-Led Feedback:

Engle incorporates this strategy regularly into her middle school language arts classroom to build student agency as well as put students in the driver's seat of their own learning. There are many benefits to student-led feedback that correlate with students seeing themselves as valued learners and thinkers. This feedback approach builds a bridge to student agency by showing kids the value of the learning process, not just the outcome of learning.

In Practice:

Engle's sixth-grade students create websites for their research projects and engage in what is called a "Research Project Website Virtual Gallery Walk," a portion of which is exemplified here with the work of a student identified with the initials "A. B." as other initialed students (on the right-hand side) provide specific comments about the project:

Research Project Website Virtual Gallery Walk

	Insert Research Project Website Link	Positive Comments What did you learn?
A.B.	https://sites.google.com/rsdmo.org/abcclaresearchproject/home	I love how organized it is. I like how you brought out how bad this issue is and could be in the future, it shows how this needs to be changed. I also like how you added a lot of pictures and videos. I like how you used a lot of text evidence to help support the rest of your paragraph. This was a wonderful website overall. – A.K. To begin, I love how you added a video to your home page. It made it more interesting and the caption for the video was spectacular! Secondly, I love how you added the background pictures to the title of every page. It makes your website look very professional. What impressed me with your website was how detailed and structured your paragraphs were. They were very informative. In the end, I thought it was smart when you wrote a paragraph about your sources and listed where you got everything from. Overall, you did an amazing job on this website! – Z.Z.

Engle presented this strategy at the Association for Middle Level Education (AMLE) annual conference in 2022. The following slide from her presentation demonstrates why details matter in student-led feedback:

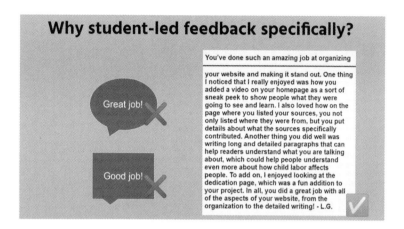

Powerful Results:

Engle distinctly remembers having tears in her eyes when one of her classes engaged in a reflective process at the end of the activity. Specifically, a student demonstrated such courage and vulnerability when she expressed how the student-led feedback she had received on her research project website gave her more confidence in herself as a writer. She shared how her classmates recognized positive traits or aspects in her writing that she didn't necessarily see and believe in herself before as a writer. That day, at the end of class, Engle remembers that same student raising her hand and asking, "Can we do this again?" Other students then chimed in, saying, "Yeah, I want to do this activity again."

Rationale:

Student-led feedback creates "win-win" learning situations for both the student receiving feedback and the student providing feedback. For the student receiving feedback from a classmate, they gain insight into what specific aspects of their writing are especially strong as well as what areas they can continue to grow in. Additionally, student-led feedback can be expressed using language and vocabulary that is more student-friendly and can even be easier to understand than receiving written or verbal feedback from the teacher who has more complex vocabulary. Furthermore, as the student giving feedback to another peer's writing, their own understanding of the writing concepts that have been taught in class solidifies. Engle believes that one of the best ways to know if a student truly demonstrates proficiency in a skill/concept is being able to successfully and effectively teach the skill/concept to someone else, and this approach empowers students as it builds their capacities and academic identities.

CHAPTER 6

Dismantling Labels and Stereotypes

Doing No Harm

For much of his time in school, Joey has been accustomed to feeling like an "other." Maybe some people are enlightened about what life is like for transgender kids, but Joey is used to being targeted for mockery or worse on a regular basis. Generally speaking, Joey will try to brush aside unintentional errors that both adults and peers make, mainly since it is already such a draining battle to be the recipient of so much bigotry and hatred.

Teachers usually represent a more supportive group where Joey is concerned, with a few notable exceptions. Still, Joey considers his classes to be a relatively safe zone, and he spends a lot of his free time working quietly in the back of classrooms when some of his nicer teachers are there anyway and let him share the space.

On this lovely autumn day, Joey is tempted to go outside during study hall, a class in which the teachers rotate and never seem to take attendance. His weather app informs him that temperatures sit in the mid-70s with a light breeze, and for a moment, Joey debates spending lunch with a few friends on the benches out front. But then, he remembers the group that sometimes walks by just to make disparaging side comments. Joey isn't really in the mood to handle that today, no matter how great the weather is. Instead, he decides to pop by Mrs. Finelli's room to see if she can let him squat there for a while.

Joey has known Mrs. Finelli for years. She's his neighbor down the block, and she is the living embodiment of what his mind conjures up when he thinks of a classic schoolroom teacher, right down to glasses sliding down her nose and the gray bun on top of her head. She comes across as strict, but there is an ever-present twinkle in her eye. She bakes amazing chocolate chip cookies, too, though she only shares them with Joey when he wanders by her house at opportune moments or helps shovel her walk in a snowstorm.

Sure enough, Mrs. Finelli is in her classroom, grading papers as she sips her morning coffee from an old plastic thermos. At the sound of the door opening, she looks up. "Joey! Why aren't you in study hall?"

"I am," Joey says, walking over to her desk. "I just want to do it here. I promise I'll be quiet."

"You would have to be," Mrs. Finelli says, pointing to a small group of students scattered around the room. "It's my off period, and they're making up a test for me."

"I won't make a sound," Joey promises. "Scout's honor."

"We both know you were never in the Scouts," Mrs. Finelli scoffs. "You don't like Mother Nature enough."

"I like sleeping indoors, that's for sure," Joey agrees. Smiling, he heads to an empty desk and gets to work on his biology homework.

He has a lot of work to focus on and the period speeds by. When the bell rings, Joey starts to head out, but Mrs. Finelli stops him. "Just wondering," she says, "did you volunteer to join the stage crew after we talked about you helping with the painting? You're so artistic."

"Right," Joey says, shifting uncomfortably from foot to foot. "Actually, I decided not to do that."

Mrs. Finelli's eyes widen, and Joey can tell she's about to unleash an unwelcome flow of objections. "Why on earth not? Joey, I vouched for you. I said what a sweet kid you are, and how helpful you would be."

Joey struggles to control his own response as she talks, but he has grown very angry, very fast. There is a constant assumption Joey fights that just because he is transgender, he must be excited to participate in anything theater related. Furthermore, the phrase "sweet kid" grates on his nerves. Joey is lots of things—snarky, wry, cooperative, insightful—but he has never considered himself "sweet." He realizes this common misperception comes from his lack of volubility in general, since being fully himself is not something that too many individuals around him are willing to accept. Instead, he keeps his mouth shut, which means a lot of people just think he's a vaguely nice person.

Now, faced with the burden of all kinds of inaccurate attributes about himself, Joey takes a deep breath. *Get out of here*, the voice inside him says. To Mrs. Finelli, he says, "Yeah, I appreciate that. I do. I just . . . yeah. I'll think about it." Without another word, he speeds out of the room, leaving Mrs. Finelli to wonder why Joey seems so reticent to join the stage crew.

Walking toward his next class, Joey is steeped in resentment. Maybe he shouldn't hang out in Mrs. Finelli's room for a while. She means well, but sometimes, that just isn't good enough. Next time he has a study hall and he can gather a few friends to join him, Joey resolves, he'll take his chances with the bench outside.

Stereotype Threat

Not all stereotypes have to be generally perceived as negative to be resented by the people to whom they are being applied. In Joey's case, his resistance is worn down by the overt prejudice that is constantly aimed at him for being transgender. When Mrs. Finelli categorizes him as a theater "type" and talks about how "sweet" he is, these seemingly innocuous labels tip Joey over the edge to the point that Mrs. Finelli's classroom (at least temporarily, if not more) no longer feels like a safe space.

The truth is, there is no such thing as a fully innocuous stereotype. People do not enjoy being misunderstood, especially when the root of the issue is an attempt to place a singular human being into a category based upon a set of observable characteristics. Even if the goal is to understand the individuals around us, which seems admirable on the surface, things get dicey when our own faulty and often unsolicited interpretations of others are verbalized or otherwise denoted.

In 1995, researchers Claude Steele and Joshua Aronson coined the term "stereotype threat" in their studies on the impact of racial bias on performance outcomes. In the study, Steele and Aronson defined stereo-type threat as "being at risk of confirming, as self-characteristic, a negative stereotype about one's group." When students are fully aware of the unfavorable stereotypes that are associated with them, they may sabotage their success by falling prey to self-fulfilling prophecies and meeting expectations that are far lower than what they are capable of accomplishing.

While the idea of stereotype threat was developed with racial bias in mind and remains by far most harmful to students of color, the danger that stereotyping presents exists for students who represent a variety of ethnicities, backgrounds, and representation and who might calibrate their academic performance to fall in line with what they feel others expect from them. As the Center for Teaching and Learning at the University of Colorado Boulder points out in an overview of stereotype threat, students who are not burdened by feeling like an "other" are far more successful with learning outcomes:

> *Students who are confident they belong in a learning community and feel valued by their teachers and peers are able to engage more fully in the classroom. With that sense of belonging, they are more likely to participate fully in discussion, build important relationships, be open to feedback and are more likely to persevere in the face of difficulty.* (2022)

Adolescents who feel secure in their sense of belonging tend to be more successful than their peers, which is helpful information for any teacher who is looking to help all students have a meaningful learning experience so that achievement increases across the board. On the other hand, when kids do not have a strong feeling of validation from a classroom community, they are more likely to engage in stereotyped behaviors that are perceived as negative.

To put a stop to the vicious cycles that stereotype threat perpetuates, it is of paramount importance to build an awareness around the insidiousness of labeling on a variety of levels. For example, many schools still support tracking students through their years of schooling starting in the very early grades, which leads to the encouragement of a system that is both inherently racist and discriminatory. For example, students are placed into academic tracks from a very young age and scheduled into the same course level year after year. More disturbing, classes that are tracked as high achieving contain fewer students of color. When students look around and see the demographic makeup of their classes, the conclusions they infer about their perceived value can have lifelong repercussions.

Beyond the inequitable methods schools employ to place students into classes that may limit their confidence and sense of capacity, the narrative that develops as a result of tracking can become disastrous. Students or classes are labeled with broad generalizations: the "smart" class, or the "slow" class. Individual kids both self-label and identify others as "nerds," or "stupid," or "suck-ups"—often because of the classes in which everyone is enrolled. While educators may truthfully express their horror at such stereotypes and their disavowal of their legitimacy, actions always speak loudest. After all, how can kids believe that teachers do not buy into the harm of stereotype threat when we also use labels, saying things like "I'm an AP teacher" instead of "I'm a teacher?"

To begin dismantling what comes as second nature to both adults and children, breaking down the systems that have automatically been embraced is essential. Labeling occurs on many levels, from building dysfunctional group dynamics to fostering unhealthy self-concept in individuals. Looking at the way class labels are created and then examining their impact on each student starts the exploratory process that leads to actionable results.

Class Labeling

"Hold on," Mr. Edwards says to the class that is trying to come into the room. "I'm still cleaning up from the first period."

Students from the previous class edge their way out into the hallway, many of them holding paper plates. When Mr. Edwards finally beckons in his second period class, they see evidence of a pancake breakfast. A griddle sits unplugged on a countertop, the trash is bursting with disposable dishes, and the room smells like maple syrup.

As everyone settles into seats, there are a few eye rolls. Mr. Edwards likes to reward his "best" class with a hot meal each month. It is February, and so far, the first period students keep winning the prize. No other classes have been rewarded the same way.

The bell rings and a boy in the second row raises his hand. Mr. Edwards calls on him immediately. "Yes, Landon?"

"Why don't we ever get the pancake breakfast?" Landon asks. "I don't understand what makes their class so much better than ours."

Mr. Edwards has already anticipated this question, and his reply is blunt. "Simple. Their behavior is better, they turn in work, and they are much more enthusiastic about what we learn. I don't have to sit here in silence waiting for someone to speak up. Anything else?"

Chastened, Landon shakes his head. From the back of the room, however, another voice suddenly joins the conversation. Rachelle has been in Mr. Edwards's class before, and she experienced this same unfairness two years ago. At the time, she didn't know what to make of a system she knew was wrong, but with plenty of opportunity for reflection, her ideas have crystallized, and she has had enough.

"I have something else," Rachelle says, speaking without raising her hand. "What if their class is just more comfortable with one another? Or what if they see that you like them more, so they participate more? It's not our fault you don't like us as much as them. It's just favoritism."

Predictably, Mr. Edwards becomes instantly annoyed. "It absolutely is not, and I don't want to hear any more. Unless you want to go to the office?"

"Actually, I do," Rachelle says. "It's better than being in here. And maybe the dean wants to hear about this. I bet she'll be interested."

Rachelle gets up, grabs her bag, and leaves the room amid the open-mouthed stares and grins from her classmates.

About time I did that, she thinks as she walks down the hallway. *That jerk deserves it.*

Beyond the stereotypes and labels teachers might assign to individual students, there is also a tendency to stigmatize groups of kids. "My last period of the day is so crazy," we might say to sympathetic colleagues. "They don't want to do anything but throw me off track." Along those lines, any number of labels might be attached to a whole class of learners, either explicitly or implicitly. Just think about how we might fill in the blank with the phrase, "This is my _____ class." Bright? Loud? Quiet? Cool? Best? Awesome? Overachieving? Insane? The list goes on and on.

Undeniably, each class develops its own personality, a distinct vibe that does not have to be tangible to be apparent. Over time, the way inside participants and outside observers perceive their class might represent a fixed point, or it might continuously shift in a more dynamic space that embraces a growth mindset. If the former, teachers and students become trapped in whatever label they have given themselves, be it positive or negative. With the latter, everyone in the classroom community recognizes that each day represents a new opportunity with results that may be unpredictable, but that are well worth the experience.

Kids take cues from adults, so avoiding any undesirable stigma around the way a class sees itself falls into the realm of teachers. Children do not have the power to make this kind of change; only adults have that ability and that responsibility. The idea of culture shift can be overwhelming, so teachers make a more immediate impact by starting with a smaller piece of how class communities are formed. Whole classes are made up of individuals, so teachers can begin by conducting an honest self-exploration of personal opinions about each student in the class and considering how these feelings contribute to a bigger picture label. Box 6.1 proposes a way to begin the process of looking at class rosters in a different light.

BOX 6.1

Roster Review

STEP ONE:

Go through rosters for each class. For each student, jot down the first descriptor that comes to mind. Note: It is okay to use the same descriptor for more than one student as needed. Then, take a step back (about a day or two) before moving on to the next step.

STEP TWO:

Consult each labeled roster. Circle descriptors that stick out as being unfair, inaccurate, or stigmatizing in any way. Too many circles may likely

begin appearing on the page, so put a star next to descriptors that contain negative connotations.

STEP THREE:

Challenge the thinking behind the identified descriptors. Which can be
reexamined with a more positive lens? Which are unjustified? How do
some of these descriptors work against student progress, even if they
are not inherently representative of deficit thinking? Reflect upon these
questions honestly.

STEP FOUR:

Identify one action that can begin to reframe the descriptors that either
explicitly or implicitly exist in each classroom. How can the descriptors
be altered or recast? Or, is there a way to disassociate students from the
descriptors? Choose one thing to change, what it will look like, and how it
can be measured. Then, check back in with this exercise in two weeks to
determine whether there has been any shift in perspective.

Incidentally, breaking whole classes into component parts is generally a
good strategy when we try to look for patterns. For example, if teachers are
conducting an exploration to determine why some students are failing a
course, zooming in on kids one at a time (known in some educational settings as "kid talk") can be enlightening. Anytime intense focus is applied
to a teaching challenge by looking at one student at a time, teachers benefit from seeing patterns emerge that might not otherwise become clear.
In the case of Box 6.1, the goal is to confront any feelings we harbor about
students, especially those that lie under the surface. Then, we challenge
that thinking and make space for a new perspective about each child in
front of us, with the ultimate purpose of considering how new perceptions
about individuals affect the entire group dynamic to make room for the
possibility of a fresh start.

Academic identity does not exist without trust. If students walk into a
classroom and they see detritus from a pancake breakfast that was given
to their peers but not themselves, there is no way they will feel anything
but resentment instead of the extrinsic motivation such reward systems

hope to achieve. Even when a situation is not quite so blatantly dysfunctional, students have a keen awareness of how their classes are labeled, regardless of whether this understanding remains unspoken. After all, kids are observant. They pick up on cues adults emit, and they meet the expectations that are set for their behavior and performance. If teachers can be more mindful of checking behavior when it comes to the thinking around each group that comes through the classroom door, we will have a far greater chance to exert a widespread positive influence on students.

Student Labeling

Nandini might be a grownup, but her childhood wounds run deep. She is the youngest of many siblings, and the only one who identifies as female. With the sexist constructs that are all too common in society, her older brothers have had a far easier path to traverse than Nandini. As a child, she was underestimated in nearly every respect of academic achievement while her brothers were celebrated for their keen intelligence, often referred to with bombastic words like "genius" or "prodigy." Nandini, on the other hand, was called "imaginative" and "spacey."

Now an adult, Nandini sees the flaws in how she was labeled throughout her formative years. Falling prey to the one-two punch of being both the youngest and the only girl, she let adults (even those who loved her) perpetuate a narrative that she lowered herself to meet. She lost interest in her schoolwork, developed a rich inner life, and tried to tune out the voices outside of her that made her seem like a well-meaning but ditsy person who liked looking out the window. All through those years, Nandini was making plans in her head, cultivating an image of who she would be. *Someday*, she would think, *You will all see what I'm made of.*

Nandini has fulfilled her own prophecies, rising to become a respected school principal, one who has great passion for trying to ensure that the students who attend her school do not feel the same way she did at their age. She knows all too well that labeling children can have long-lasting, catastrophic effects, a thought that education scholar Sanya Pelini (2022) echoes when she writes: "Labeling kids not only shapes their personality, it also shapes the relationship you develop with them well beyond the childhood years" (para. 3). While Nandini realizes that a strong sense of internal drive helped her change the narrative others created for her, there are so many children who do not have that same satisfactory outcome. Nandini considers it her life's purpose to help them.

For anyone who works in education like Nandini, there is an added awareness around how students are best set up to learn. Teachers cannot be as instrumental at undoing the damage that is caused at home when children are labeled by the people in their personal lives, but they can do their best not to perpetuate harmful paradigms within school walls. Some more obvious strategies include resisting the urge to compare kids to one another, not attaching adjectives to a child in conversation, and focusing on the ideas they share more than their personal inclinations. For example, very few children appreciate hearing: "You're so quiet! Speak up more in class." Instead, it is far more encouraging to say something like: "The paragraph you wrote about the bystander effect was so thoroughly researched. I'd love to discuss it more." Then, a so-called "quiet" student is far more likely to engage in subsequent classes, knowing that the teacher already likes what they have to say.

While it is hardly revelatory to point out that students will be deeply influenced by the way adults perceive them to the point that their behavior changes, the impact of labeling on outcomes cannot be overstated. In 1968, social psychologist Robert Rosenthal and elementary school principal Lenore Jacobson wrote an article entitled "Pygmalion in the Classroom" in which they detailed an experiment they conducted in a school. For the study, they informed a group of teachers that they would be working with students throughout the year who they identified by name and labeled "spurters," which meant that these students were expected to make quick academic gains. This information was utterly false in that the students were selected at random, but Rosenthal and Jacobsen kept that nugget of information to themselves. The teachers were cautioned to keep what they had been told confidential, but to monitor the progress of their student group closely throughout the year.

What happened next is not difficult to guess. The identified "spurters" performed significantly better than the control group of their peers in the same classes, even though there was no genuine difference in ability driving their success. As Rosenthal and Jacobson (1968) so succinctly put it: "When teachers expected that certain children would show greater intellectual development, those children did show greater intellectual development" (p. 20). Teacher beliefs around student capability led to measurable achievement growth for the identified students, while their classmates were likely dismissed without the beneficial label of being deemed "spurters."

It is also not difficult to imagine that throughout those months of the experiment, teachers were attaching labels to their "spurters" that may have been highly visible to everyone in the room and discouraging to kids who were labeled quite differently. Perhaps teachers used words like "smart," "bright," "capable," or "driven" to describe the students who had already been pegged as geniuses in the making. Maybe other kids were told they were "lazy," "stubborn," or "incorrigible." Even in the absence of overt negative labeling, the non-"spurter" group would have been able to easily discern their exclusion from a club of "smart" kids. Children are highly susceptible to believing the opinions of adults, especially those in positions of power, and they are also observant. While labels can exist on a more obvious plane, they also occur stealthily. Either way, students are no less aware of them. Table 6.1 provides three levels of labeling to consider with examples that are attached to kids on a personal level (either at school or at home), those that occur more commonly in a classroom setting, and those that exist under the surface.

TABLE 6.1

Level 1: Personal	assertive, confident, cooperative, incompetent, introverted, lazy, loner, outgoing, popular, sociable, talkative
Level 2: Academic	average, bright, clown, geeky, genius, nerdy, overachieving, sharp, slacker, slow, studious, underachieving
Level 3: Stealth	angry, brave, eccentric, emotional, forgetful, interesting, oppositional, quiet, shy, sweet, talented, vocal

Regardless of whether a label is visible or not, the damage that results from being placed into a category can be irrevocable. Even potentially flattering labels trap kids in ways that are harmful. For example, when a child is consistently held to high academic standards with the expectation of near perfectionism, any perceived external success might occur at the expense of mental health. Seemingly innocuous labels like "quiet" or "shy" cause enormous resentment among students who are simply uncomfortable in certain settings, or who do not wish to speak up all the time. And of course, overtly harmful labels usually accomplish their intended result.

To undo the damage labeling causes, awareness is not enough. Teachers must actively dismantle the systems that lead to labeling students and that allow stereotyping to exist unchecked. Otherwise, classrooms cannot become the safe and trusting spaces that are necessary for student academic identity to grow and flourish.

Dismantling Harmful Norms

Mara sits in the cafeteria at lunchtime, furiously scribbling answers to her math homework on the page in front of her. She jumps slightly as Janelle, her best friend, bumps her on the shoulder as she slides into a seat at their customary lunch table.

"What're you doing?" Janelle asks, popping a French fry into her mouth. She makes a face as she bites down. "Ew, gross. Soggy."

Without looking up, Mara replies, "I'm doing my algebra homework. I didn't have time last night."

"Of course you didn't, Slacker."

This time, Mara does look up. "Could you please not call me that?"

"Why not? It's true. You never do your homework. Here, have some of my fries. They're disgusting."

"Yeah, I'm going to refuse that tempting offer," Mara says, rolling her eyes. "And I was up late doing my other homework. That doesn't make me a slacker."

"That's exactly what it makes you," Janelle says. "I'm in the IB program and I have a million more things than you to do, and somehow, I get it all done. You're just making excuses."

"Whatever," Mara grumbles, looking back down at her homework.

After a few minutes of eating in silence, Janelle looks at Mara. "I'm bored," she announces. I'm going to find someone who did their homework last night to talk to. Later, Slacker."

"You suck," Mara calls after her, but it's too late. Janelle is already gone, casing the cafeteria. She left her tray behind, and Mara picks up a fry. She forgot to pack her lunch, so she's pretty hungry. She takes a bite and makes a face. Janelle was right—they're not worth eating.

Once again, Mara picks up her pencil and looks at her math homework with a huge sigh. She might be filling out the paper in front of her, but she has no idea whether the answers are close to correct. When the teacher was demonstrating problems in class yesterday, she didn't really understand what to do as she dutifully copied down what he wrote on the board.

Oh well, she thinks, finishing the last problem and sticking it into her folder. *At least I finished it before class. Maybe Janelle has a point. I am a slacker.*

Labeling is so pervasive in school culture that it occurs ubiquitously in a variety of interpersonal reactions: student-to-student, teacher-to-student, teacher-to-teacher, and teacher-to-administrator (and vice versa). While Mara might want to rethink her close friendship with a friend who calls her "Slacker," people generally allow the labels that others attach without much pushback, especially when intentions are perceived as being good. As we all know, however, intent does not really matter when the result is injurious.

To start dismantling hurtful stereotypes right away, one technical fix that gets momentum moving in the right direction is to give added attention to the use of adjectives. When teachers describe the students in our classes, we attach words to their identities, either in our minds or in overt expression. We might chat with a colleague and say, "Oh, I have Kerry this year. She's quite a go-getter, isn't she?" Or, we might look at a student in the back row of our class and think, *Of course Wylie is taking out his phone again. He's such a disappointment.* Whether we verbalize our thoughts or not, they are more transparent than we believe. Perhaps teachers beam when Kerry walks into the room and engage her in conversation, or shake their heads ever so slightly when Wylie stares at his device. Thoughts lead to observable behavior, and kids know what teachers think of them.

To start retraining our brains, teachers can work with students on the adjective exercise featured in Box 6.2, which is designed to both build awareness and redirect thinking. This process, which is a riff on the traditional college application recommendation process that asks teachers to describe students with individual adjectives, allows everyone to dig a lot deeper into the power of descriptive words.

BOX 6.2

Three Adjectives

Today, you will brainstorm three adjectives that best describe yourself beyond what is obvious to the eye.

Follow this process:

1. Make a list of adjectives that others might use to describe you. Circle any you agree with, and cross out any you disagree with.
2. Of the adjectives you circled, take a moment to question what you see. Are those the most apt words, or can you do better?
3. Start building your own list that includes complimentary adjectives that are not yet on the paper. Feel free to put down any adjectives that come to mind, from more obvious choices to less apparent thoughts.
4. Take a few extra minutes to think of empowering adjectives that might not sit on the surface, but that run deeper to accurately describe the essence of YOU.
5. Now . . . the hard part! Of the whole list you just compiled, pick the three adjectives that are best at providing a glimpse into who you really are. Write the three final choices at the bottom of your page and await next steps from the teacher!

When students build their adjective lists, the intent is to see themselves in a more profound light, one that showcases the best of themselves. Teachers who want to increase the affirming power of this exercise may wish to supply students with large strips of colorful paper and markers, upon which they can write their chosen adjectives and post them on a designated wall space. That way, when students fall into less confident frames of mind, there is a consistent physical reminder of the best part of themselves right in front of them. Another option for teachers is to collect the adjectives and then mindfully use them with students throughout the school year to affirm their confidence.

As part of an overt exploration into challenging and dismantling labels, the next step in prioritizing a classroom community that has developed mutual trust is to transparently question some of the less helpful labels that have afflicted everyone over the years. In Table 6.2, the teacher guides students to "flip" categorized labels that are frequently placed upon adolescents. In this activity, kids share their best thinking in a safe space, helping one another by presenting alternate points of view that shift damaging norms and turn them into assets.

TABLE 6.2

Confronting the Norm: Flipping Labels	
Loaded and Unproductive	Neutral and Productive
Apathetic: lazy, bored, slow	Not yet: engaged, inspired, actively learning
Disruptive: rude, mean, angry	Not yet: collaborative, communicative
Invisible: quiet, shy, introverted	Not yet: visibly thinking, contributing

With just these few examples in Table 6.2, students will see that by reframing what are commonly seen as deficits with the growth mindset approach of "not yet," their behavior is reframed as changeable. With activities like the ones featured in Table 6.2 and Box 6.2, students also begin to understand where they have been unproductively labeled throughout their young lives. Even more powerful, they may see that whether an assigned stereotype is perceived as a benefit, detriment, or even perhaps with neutrality, so many labels ultimately act as forces for harm. Once this realization has sunk in, the next step is for teachers to incorporate more explicit strategies into instructional repertoire that help students not just see their learning with a new perspective, but also reconsider their own academic identities.

Instructional Accountability

Trina sometimes reflects that the healthiest thing she ever did for herself was get away from home for college.

When she thinks this way, she doesn't want anyone to misunderstand her. Her parents are kind and loving. She is close with her siblings, though they are identical twins and therefore more bonded with one another than with her. The fact that growing up in her house was challenging had more to do with her own insecurities than anything else, but now a junior at a renowned university far away, Trina sees a whole new pathway for herself that she never would have dreamed of just a couple of years before.

Growing up, Trina was what those conversant in sports lingo might call a "utility player" in that she could do many things very well. While she loved to read more than anything, her math skills were so advanced that her parents seized on the praise teachers heaped upon Trina and enrolled her in enriched STEM courses. Words like "brilliant," "rare," and "exceptional" were often used to describe her, which in retrospect Trina finds sexist. After all, there were any number of girls in her class who could likely do just as well, had they been encouraged the same way. She sees that now, but back then, she basked in the praise and wound up in a specialized magnet program in high school, building expertise in robotics and competing in math tournaments with mainly male peers.

When she got into a university program that few students overall get into, not to mention women, Trina's parents were ecstatic. She also got a hefty pre-med scholarship that covered the majority of her tuition. For a while, Trina rode the wave of success along with her family, ignoring a nagging doubt buried deep within her. That is, until she arrived at school and spent a semester taking courses that were okay enough, but that did not excite her.

One day, Trina wandered into the campus coffee shop later than usual. She had a long night of studying ahead and she felt a sudden urge for a very strong mocha with extra chocolate sauce. As she got in line, a voice coming from a microphone behind her caught her attention and Trina turned around. There was a woman about her age, reading her poetry aloud to a small gathering of students who were clearly fellow writers. As they snapped their approval at the close of each poem, their camaraderie with one another was almost tangible.

It was, Trina reflected as she collected her drink, very different from the cutthroat environment she had so far encountered in her pre-med program. This group of students seemed to appreciate and support one another, rather than being obsessed with outranking one another's accomplishments. The woman up front sat down and made way for another poet, and Trina found herself perching on a stool to listen. *Just for a few minutes*, she told herself.

Those few minutes turned into several nights, then a course in poetry, and finally, a minor in English that includes as many writing courses she can squeeze into her packed schedule. Trina knows that her scholarship depends on her completing the pre-med program, but she hasn't found a way to tell her parents that after undergraduate school ends, she plans to apply for an MFA program in creative writing. Sooner rather than later, Trina will break the unwelcome news, and while she is hardly looking forward to her family's disappointment, she is proud of herself. She has removed herself from a situation that involved others (however well-meaning) labeling her as something that never sat fully comfortably. Now that Trina no longer dreads many years of med school, internship, and residency, she is excited for the years ahead. Inevitably, there will be struggles as she figures out how to support herself, but for the first time, she finally feels as though she is headed in the right direction.

Trina has been lucky enough to get some distance from a situation that did not serve her own academic identity and course-correct with a plan that suits her needs far better than what others would have chosen for her. Not all students have the same benefit of both removing themselves from a less ideal situation and having the confidence to change their own lives. As such, it is the teacher's job to empower students to build their confidence within instructional spaces. Then, students can transfer the skills they learn in the classroom to life outside of school.

When teachers seek to change student perspectives, the role of explicitness is frequently underestimated. For example, if the goal is to help students understand the benefit of a growth mindset approach, we may use language like "yet" to subtly indicate that while learning targets have not been met at this time, that doesn't mean students will not achieve them in the future. However, without specifically teaching kids about what it means to apply effective effort and hard work to reaching a higher level of achievement, they will only see growth mindset as a muddy concept that doesn't have any real application to their lives.

Similarly, if teachers want students to understand that their scholarship has value, we must explicitly teach them what that looks like. Box

6.3 denotes very specific ways teachers can denote the goal of building academic identity with students so that everyone holds shared accountability for reaching a more ideal state.

BOX 6.3

Strategies for Teaching Academic Identity

- Give students age-appropriate reading materials, podcasts, or videos about growth mindset, including the elements of effective effort and how to be resourceful.
- Reaffirm that everybody feels like an outsider sometimes to normalize feelings of "otherness."
- Be transparent about the criteria for success on all assignments, so that students connect performance to a product and not to themselves.
- Tell students explicitly that grades and numbers do not define their identities, and explain why.
- When students make contributions, consistently affirm their responses by assigning value to ideas, and explain the rationale for seeing validity in each response.
- On a regular basis, ask students to identify what they are doing well, and explain that they have a more balanced perspective when they can pinpoint their strengths.
- Prioritize collectivism over individualism by creating group structures that are not connected to evaluation (i.e., grades), but that help students see the benefit of combined intelligence.

As part of teaching students that they hold the key to seeing themselves differently, it also falls upon teachers to lead instruction that reinforces validating messages. When students get the message that teachers do not believe in their intelligence, any work that is done to change the narrative around confidence falls apart. To ensure that unintentional mixed messages do not dominate instructional time, one key to maintaining overt belief in students is to keep them working with appropriate grade-level content rather than accidentally or intentionally providing remediation for skills or standards that exist in prior years of schooling.

In a pandemic recovery period that seems to be extending longer than expected (at least, at the time of this writing in late 2022), teachers have felt the understandable and unyielding pressure to ensure that students who have experienced a significant degree of learning disruption are able to meet curriculum goals by the close of each school year. However, in the desire to be helpful, some teachers have taken students an unintentional step backward by lowering expectations for performance. As Alice Wiggins (2020), the vice president for Instructional Design at UnboundEd writes, "providing support for our students starts with an asset orientation. We begin by considering what our students already know, their cultural funds of knowledge, and their prior experiences that can support them in the task or text." Rather than look for deficits in knowledge, it first makes sense to figure out what students already have a handle on. If not, teachers will make all kinds of erroneous assumptions about content acquisition.

Furthermore, when teachers undervalue what students can do by lowering the bar for achievement, that lack of faith is visible. Suppose I assign a four-paragraph essay and I see a student struggling to complete even a few sentences. Assuming the student in question does not have accommodations for special needs by law, in which case I am required to offer modifications to the assignment, the approach I select to help the student must reflect support, not enabling. For example, if I ask the student to just write one paragraph and never ask for the remaining three, I have modified the work and lowered the expectation for the student so that they are no longer meeting the standard of instruction, which is inappropriate. Instead, my job is to provide scaffolding to get the student to the required standard, such as providing some sentence starters or frames to get the process underway, or perhaps giving them a brainstorming protocol to get ideas flowing. However, no matter what supports I put in place to assist the student, the end goal remains the same for them as for everyone else in the class, which is to meet the grade-level expectation for performance and write all four paragraphs.

In addition to showing students that adults believe in them through the way we teach, it is important to not rely on intuition. Otherwise, the instruction teachers design cannot authentically meet the needs of students. Following the "feedback on feedback" protocol outlined in Chapter

4, asking students questions like the ones displayed in Box 6.4 helps everyone to stay mindful of the mutual goal of building academic identity, and recenters instruction that may otherwise stray too far from the point of effectiveness.

BOX 6.4

Student Voice Survey: Question Bank

- Do you feel validated as a learner in this class? Are your ideas respected and valued? If so, how do you know? If not, what does that look or feel like?
- When your teacher asks questions, are you comfortable providing a response? Explain.
- Does your teacher believe that you can meet high expectations? How do you know?
- Is your teacher excited to discuss ideas with you? Explain.
- How has your work continued to improve so far this year? What are you working on next?
- When you think about reaching goals, which ones are more attainable? What do you find frustrating, and why?
- What is working for your learning in this class?
- What is getting in the way of your learning?
- How do your classmates play a role in how you are learning? Would another type of interaction be more productive?
- Is your learning style being accommodated most of the time, some of the time, or never? Explain.
- After today's class, what are your lingering questions?

The questions offered in Box 6.4 as options for student voice are a place to start when teachers seek to discover how kids feel about their learning. The continuing benefit of gathering student feedback is not just that it's informative, but that the process can also vary based on needs. A teacher might choose to ask just one or two of the questions contained in Box 6.4 depending on timely factors, or when a semester or unit ends, it might be better to provide a more comprehensive feedback survey. Either way, sharing results and next steps with students is integral to cementing their scholarly presence in the classroom.

Throughout this chapter, we have examined a multitude of ideas and strategies for the very intricate process of chipping away at deep-seated stereotypes and labels. While implementing these ideas is a start, more meaningful work lies in the consistent and aware application of practices that work against bias. Dismantling labels and stereotypes to make way for healthier norms is complex work that requires a lot of unpacking, but the effort is well worth the results. Students may get lucky in their older years like Trina and figure out who they are despite some of the labels that have plagued them for so many years, but nobody can assume that will be the case. By working intentionally to interrupt all the ways students are boxed into places they never chose to be, teachers have a more direct pathway to building academic identity through skillful instructional methods.

Cross-Content Strategy

Music, Middle School
Contributor: Adria Hoffman

Context: Consuming and Performing versus Creating
When most people think of music in schools, performances are often the most common experience. Even in elementary schools across the U.S., where there is so much happening beyond performance, the concerts, plays, and musicals are what families, community members, and even other teachers first think of.

At the secondary level, there has certainly been greater diversity of course offerings over the past two decades, but most music students enroll in ensemble-focused electives. In many of these settings, the implicit message is that learning to perform music written by others is most important. Rarely do learners have the opportunity to create something original that empowers their own identity as musicians. As a classroom teacher, Hoffman wants to provide learners with the opportunity to create music, not only to consume and perform it. Below are three approaches that can easily be adapted to any developmental level.

Approach 1:

Begin with feelings. After all, everyone has big feelings from time to time!

First, ask learners to think of a big feeling and then ask them to choose colors that represent those feelings. Teachers might ask older students to think of a time when they felt strong emotions and, as the situation unfolded, how their feelings changed.

PROMPTS:

What colors might represent the different feelings? Was there a linear path, or timeline, along which the colors changed? Or did you feel as though you moved back and forth among varied emotions? After visualizing it (using digital of manual coloring tools), ask learners to find various tones and timbres that represent the emotions or that "sound like the colors."

EXTENSIONS:

This can begin an exploration of creating sounds and colors, visual representations, and multimedia content. Students might learn a melody on a primary instrument, but make recommendations about arrangements for different instruments, for example. They could also begin to create emotional "palettes" of sorts, serving as the foundation for larger creative exploration.

Approach 2:

Begin with rhythm—beats, rhymes, and spoken word. We hear rhythm all around us.

Using body percussion, invite learners to improvise over a very basic rhythmic motif. They might even recommend their favorite song, social media, or commercial. A recognizable motif to utilize is to have the group pat on their knees while the improvised ideas are tried, popcorn style, by one learner at a time, creating a collaborative, creative learning experience.

PROMPTS:

Who has a song they just can't get out of their head? Who else knows this one? Can you all sing it and we can all find the rhythm underneath? Let's keep that rhythm going on our knees. I'm going to clap a few beats over it. Who has another beat? Let's pass the "mic" (ahem, hand claps) around!

EXTENSIONS:

Learners can then work in smaller groups to build out their ideas. Some may feel free to create multiple layers while others might need some examples before they feel safe enough to try this. By returning to their motifs for each subsequent class, learners will organically extend their musical ideas. Teaching them to focus on cues and to use whatever cues work for them in the moment will help them create clear entrances, cut-offs, and transitions.

Approach 3:

Begin with literature.

Invite learners to bring a short story, poem, or other excerpt meaningful to them or to someone they know. They might share a family member's favorite poem, for example.

PROMPTS:

What is a word or phrase that really grabs your attention here? What surprises you by the language choices the author makes? What emotions do they convey? Close your eyes for a moment and picture the landscape described here. Imagine a screenwriter turning this into a movie or series. You're going to write/create the background music.

EXTENSIONS:

The prompts above provide a few options for extensions, such as creating the background music or perhaps beginning with a voicing or timbre, then building from there. Teachers might begin with a known musical motif and give learners the freedom to create variations. They might first vary the instrumentation or voicing. Or they might begin with the time signature or even the genre. Making a classical piece sound like jazz or sampling a motif and creating a larger work around it can provide starting points for those overwhelmed by the idea of creating music without parameters so they can have fun with the process while finding their voices.

Conclusion:
The Years Beyond

Preservice week is always a whirlwind. Schools, silent for so long over the summer, burst with activity as teachers attend meetings, decorate their classrooms, and plan lessons together for students who are arriving in just a few days.

For Yolanda, the pace of this unusual week is familiar. Now in her 24th year of teaching, she is well-versed in the process of getting back into the rhythm of things. On this first day of preservice, she is already in her classroom bright and early to start hanging up posters before the general session begins in the auditorium.

Sooner than she'd like, an announcement comes over the P.A. system at 8 o'clock. "Attention, teachers. Welcome back! Breakfast is served in the cafeteria, so please come on down. Our meeting will begin at 8:30 sharp."

Reluctantly, Yolanda stops what she's working on and puts her precious roll of blue tape (a hot commodity) securely in her bag, which she hefts onto her shoulder. She wanders toward the cafeteria, waving at friends and colleagues who pass by.

The breakfast spread is lovely, manned by kind parent volunteers who have sacrificed their early morning to show appreciation for the school staff. Yolanda picks out a selection of fruit and helps herself to a cup of tepid coffee from a large steel urn. She scans the cafeteria, finds a table that is slowly filling with members of her department and heads toward them.

As she puts her plate down, she suddenly hears a voice behind her. "Mrs. James! Hi!"

Yolanda turns around and it takes a moment for her to place the person who is speaking. Katy, a former student, stands in front of her, but it's been several years since Yolanda has seen her, so long that it takes a moment to remember her name. Relieved that she can recall that much information, Yolanda smiles. "Katy! My goodness. What on earth brings you here?"

Katy holds up a bright, shiny new staff ID card. "I'm a teacher now. I got my master's in teaching and interned last year. I'll be in the math department with you!"

"Wow," Yolanda says, trying to remember how long it's been. "That is such good news! You're making me feel old. Remind me, when did I teach you?"

"I graduated six years ago," Katy says. "And I'm really glad you're here. I never really got a chance to tell you how much you changed my life, and now I can do that."

"Me?"

Katy nods. "You might not realize this, but I had zero confidence about math when I came to your class. I said all the things kids sometimes say— that I was bad at it and it wasn't my thing. You were always so welcoming and you helped me understand why the way I tried to solve problems worked, or why they didn't, and you didn't judge me. You actually seemed to enjoy it when we made mistakes. I never forgot that."

Yolanda is usually a fairly matter-of-fact person, but she feels her eyes welling up a little. Her hand goes to her heart. "I'm so touched. I'm not sure what to say. Just . . . what you say means a lot to me. It's hard to explain how much."

Satisfied, Katy shakes her head. "You don't have to say anything. I just needed you to know that you changed my life. I majored in math, and then my experience in your class made me want to be a teacher. I want to help other kids the way you helped me."

One tear spills over onto Yolanda's cheek, and she quickly wipes it away. "That is the loveliest thing I've heard in a long time, Katy. Thank you."

Katy nods her acknowledgement, sticking her hands in her pockets and looking around. She suddenly looks a little at a loss about what to do next. Seeing her unease, Yolanda jumps in. "Are you planning on getting something to eat?"

"Already did," Katy says, pulling a napkin-wrapped bagel out of her large bag. "I was just looking for a seat."

"You have a seat," Yolanda says, pulling out the chair next to hers. "You're a math teacher now. Join us."

Katy and Yolanda sit down, turning their attention to colleagues seated around the table. One of the more seasoned math teachers leans toward Yolanda to whisper in her ear. "I was eavesdropping," he confesses. "Nicely done, Yo!"

Yolanda takes a sip her coffee and winces, wishing she'd stopped at a Starbucks on the way in. "Thanks. It's why we're here, right?"

"Yep," he confirms.

They join the rest of the table's conversation, sharing their summer stories and hopes for the coming year. Yolanda soaks it all in, realizing that even if the subpar coffee won't give her the pick-me-up she needs this morning, talking to Katy has energized her. She can't wait for this school year to start.

The Writing Gateway

Students express themselves in all kinds of ways. Some love to write, littering notebook pages or online documents with their musings. Others paint, or excel in athletics, or emote onstage in school plays. Then, there are kids who might solve complex mathematical formulas or organize social awareness initiatives, showing their passion for solving climate change or engaging in political action at an earlier age than some of their peers. For too many preteens and teens, however, teachers never see evidence of inner drive, mainly because there might be no provided arena within classrooms to make space for hidden talent or skill.

The bulk of the strategies woven throughout this book have been explicitly connected to the act of written expression. By now, it should be clear that the phrase "writing activity" in the context of these chapters does not denote some of the common assumptions about what constructing compositions for English class entails, such as the mental image of students working on five-paragraph essays with established formulaic structures ad nauseam. Rather, the consistent thinking behind each strategy shared throughout these pages is to provide an accessible, engaging gateway for student expression regardless of any individual child's affinity for the written word. To put it plainly, all students who write are writers—and all students who learn are scholars.

Regardless of how well pathways to learning are opened through the process of engaging more deeply in the written realm, being equipped to transfer skills in all four language domains (reading, writing, speaking, and listening) beyond one subject and extend newfound academic identity to content areas in which students have a more vested interest is beneficial. Future scientists, mathematicians, performers, or athletes may not be able to automatically transfer a sense of confidence from one content area to another without seeing clear connections between their own sense of self and each field of study. Writing activities can certainly be implemented in a science class, for example, but what then? What can teachers do next to more explicitly tie course outcomes to maintaining academic identity?

The cross-content strategies that are shared throughout this book exemplify a deep-seated belief in the value of collective intelligence over individual knowledge. Rather than try and find theoretical ways to brainstorm methods that support academic identity in multiple content areas by digging into books or articles, it felt more relevant and practical to ask secondary teachers in a variety of content areas to share some of their most effective strategies for engaging students in work that builds confidence and efficacy in each specified subject. The tools that are provided at the close of each chapter are not hypothetical; they are practical. They have been implemented consistently, with real kids, with success. With teacher experts weighing in to share their best thinking, the collective benefit is evident as we learn from one another. The beauty of the best professional development—the teacher down the hall—is that it can be replicated or adapted in any school building to meet the ever-changing needs of students.

Becoming and Belonging

This is the book I have most wanted to write, the one that has felt the most personal and the most healing.

In the spring of 2022, when *Teach More, Hover Less* came out, the very week of my first book publication was overshadowed by the death of my beloved father, who taught English at Indiana University for nearly 40 years. He was a brilliant lecturer and very much a teacher of his time—someone whose keen insight was put on display as what we now call a "sage on the stage." Unlike many other teachers of his era, however, he never discounted or disregarded the possibility that there might be other legitimate ways to conduct instruction.

When I became a high school teacher, he was supportive. "Your job is much harder than mine," he would say, and not without truth. He taught a few classes a week to compliant, eager graduate students while I taught five classes in one day to teenagers who had not elected to spend time with me of their own volition. Earlier in my career, I would ask for his advice as I developed lessons. He is the one who planted the seed for the virtual rhetoric lesson featured earlier in this book by helping me connect the Bruegel painting to the Auden poem. I also brought him into my classes as a "guest lecturer" or simply an observer, and my students connected to him instantly. Lecturer or not, he was a dynamic teacher who knew how to wind a class around his little finger. In fact, *The New York Times* reporter William Grimes (2007) provided an apt encomium of my father's teaching in a book review of a Shakespeare anthology. He wrote:

> The most compelling production of Antony and Cleopatra *that I can recall took place not in a theater but in a classroom. From a distance of nearly 40 years, I can still hear the basso profundo of Melvin Plotinsky at Indiana University declaiming some of Shakespeare's most stirring lines, interspersed with brilliant commentary that began at 10 a.m. sharp and concluded precisely 45 minutes later. At that point, the thoroughly intimidating Professor Plotinsky would reach into the pocket of his suit jacket, pull out a silver cigarette case, and exit stage left, leaving me slack-jawed with amazement.* (para. 1)

To this day, I'm grateful to William Grimes, whom I have never met, for such a lovely portrait of the father I loved so much.

With such an academically gifted parent, it was painfully noticeable that I was less motivated to succeed in school at a younger age. After my first book came out, I spoke with so many people about my own student experiences going back to what is often a traumatic time for so many children: middle school. In my preteen years, I did not have a strong inner belief in my own intelligence. Teachers compared me unfavorably to my siblings, classes were unengaging, and I lived in a community that seemed to find me invisible. It didn't help that my peers were unkind, labeling me as anything from an underachiever to simply not cool enough to be worthy of their time.

The wounds formed during that time still exist within me in the form of light scarring, but I built a new story for myself that began in high school and gained traction into adulthood. When my father saw my newfound dedication to education, he was initially surprised. But then, I explained my purpose: to help kids who were invisible, underestimated, misunderstood, and to use the empathy I had as a less valued member of the school community for the purpose of empowering all students to see themselves differently. As my career gained momentum, my father would occasionally say: "Who would have thought this is what you'd become?" And I would answer him honestly. "I did. I thought it would, because I believed it could happen."

But then, not all children have the same experience, and some are wounded so badly they cannot recover as they get older to become the people that, deep down, they know they could be if the stars would align the right way. That is why building academic identity in all classrooms is so important. It's not okay for anyone to feel like an "other," even some of the time. When kids know their ideas have value, that belief follows them wherever they go, for however long they walk this earth.

The human experience is one of adaptation. In education, teachers are given the distinct gift of starting anew with each year, each unit, even each day. If readers learn nothing else from these pages, my hope is that they walk away with this one affirming thought: *I have the power to change the world around me for good.* Live this out through instruction, through teaching students they have the exact same capacity, and through being known as the teacher who welcomes and openly values all voices, ideas, and perspectives. Only then can we fulfill a ubiquitous purpose for all educators to, as Mahatma Gandhi put it, "Be the change you wish to see in the world." The future may not be certain, but teachers want nothing more than for students to believe in their capacity to be valuable contributors to the societies they inhabit, both in the present and in the time to come.

References

Berger, R. (2021). Our kids are not broken. *The Atlantic*. Retrieved from https://www.theatlantic.com/ideas/archive/2021/03/how-to-get-our-kids-back-on-track/618269/

Brame, C. (2016). *Active learning*. Vanderbilt University Center for Teaching. Retrieved from https://cft.vanderbilt.edu/wp-content/uploads/sites/59/Active-Learning.pdf

Brenneman, R. (2016). Gallup student poll finds engagement in school dropping by grade level. *Education Week*. Retrieved from https://www.edweek.org/leadership/gallup-student-poll-finds-engagement-in-school-dropping-by-grade-level/2016/03

Bronson, P. (2009). How not to talk to your kids. *New York*. Retrieved from https://nymag.com/news/features/27840/

Center for Teaching and Learning (2022). Stereotype threat. University of Colorado Boulder. Retrieved from https://www.colorado.edu/center/teaching-learning/inclusivity/stereotype-threat

Chohan, S. K. (2010). Whispering selves and reflective transformations in the internal dialogue of teachers and students. *Journal of Invitational Theory and Practice, 16*. Retrieved from https://files.eric.ed.gov/fulltext/EJ942555.pdf

Deslauriers, L., McCarty, L.S., Miller, K., & Kestin, G. (2019). Measuring actual learning versus feeling of learning in response to being actively engaged in the classroom. *PNAS, 116*(39). Retrieved from https://www.pnas.org/doi/10.1073/pnas.1821936116

Flowers, B. (1981) Madman, architect, carpenter, judge: Roles and the writing process. *National Council of Teachers of English, 50*(7), 834–836,

Goodwin, B. & Miller, J. (2012). Research says/good feedback is targeted, specific, timely. *ASCD, 70*(1). Retrieved from https://www.ascd.org/el/articles/research-says-good-feedback-is-targeted-specific-timely

Grimes, W. (2007). Keeping the faith with Shakespeare. *The New York Times*. Retrieved from https://www.nytimes.com/2007/04/27/books/27shak.html

Hattie, J. & Timperley, H. (2007). The power of feedback. *Review of Educational Research, 77*(1), 81–112. Retrieved from http://www.columbia.edu/~mvp19/ETF/Feedback.pdf

Hammond, Z. (2015). *Culturally responsive teaching and the brain: Promoting authentic engagement and rigor among culturally and linguistically diverse students*. Corwin.

Hernández, L. E. & Darling-Hammond, L. (2022). Creating identity-safe schools and classrooms. *Learning Policy Institute*. Retrieved from https://doi.org/10.54300/165.102

Lahey, J. (2013). Introverted kids need to learn to speak up at school. *The Atlantic*. Retrieved from https://www.theatlantic.com/national/archive/2013/02/introverted-kids-need-to-learn-to-speak-up-at-school/272960/

O'Keefe, P., Lee H. Y., & Chen, P. (2021). Changing students' beliefs about learning can unveil their potential. *SAGE Journals, 8*(1), 84–91. Retrieved from https://journals.sagepub.com/doi/epub/10.1177/2372732220984173

Pelini, S. (2022). Labeling kids: Why we need to stop. *Raising Independent Kids*. Retrieved from https://raising-independent-kids.com/labeling-kids-why-we-need-to-stop/

Plotinsky, M. (2022). 3 strategies to reduce student burnout. *Edutopia*. Retrieved from https://www.edutopia.org/article/3-strategies-reduce-student-burnout

Plotinsky, M. (2022). *Teach more, hover less: How to stop micromanaging your secondary classroom*. Norton.

Ritchhart, R., Church, M., Morrison. K., & Perkins, D. (2011). *Making thinking visible: How to promote engagement, understanding, and independence for all learners.* Jossey-Bass.

Roberts, P. M. (1958). *How to say nothing in 500 words.* Retrieved from https://www.defmacro.org/HowtoSayNothingin500Words.pdf

Rosenthal, R. & Jacobson, L. (1968). Pygmalion in the classroom. *The Urban Review 3,* 16–20. https://doi.org/10.1007/BF02322211

Shevrin Venet, A. (2018). The how and why of trauma-informed teaching. *Edutopia.* Retrieved from https://www.edutopia.org/article/how-and-why-trauma-informed-teaching

Spencer, J. (2022). Encouraging introverts to speak up in school. Retrieved from https://quietrev.com/encouraging-introverts-to-speak-up-in-school/

Steele, C. M., & Aronson, J. (1995). Stereotype threat and the intellectual test performance of African Americans. *Journal of Personality and Social Psychology, 69*(5), 797–811. Retrieved from https://doi.org/10.1037/0022-3514.69.5.797

Seuss, D. (1957). *The cat in the hat.* Houghton Mifflin.

Terada, Y. (2019). Students think lectures are best, but research suggests they're wrong. *Edutopia.* Retrieved from https://www.edutopia.org/article/students-think-lectures-are-best-research-suggests-they-re-wrong

Weiner, B. (1972). Attribution theory, achievement motivation, and the educational process. *Review of Educational Research, 42*(2), 203–215. Retrieved from https://www.researchgate.net/publication/270334287_Attribution_Theory_Achievement_Motivation_and_the_Educational_Process

Wiggins, A. (2020). Supports vs. modifications: What's the difference? *UnboundEd.* Retrieved from https://www.unbounded.org/blog/supports-vs-modifications-whats-the-difference

Wiggins, G. (2012). Seven keys to effective feedback. *ASCD, 70*(1). Retrieved from http://www.ascd.org/el/articles/seven-keys-to-effective-feedback

Index

Note: Italicized page locators refer to figures; tables are noted with a *t*.

About the Author

Miriam Plotinsky is an author and instructional specialist who addresses challenges in both teaching and leading across schools with a wide range of differentiated needs. A strong advocate for student-centered learning, she provides coaching and professional development for teachers and administrators. She has written *Teach More, Hover Less: How to Stop Micromanaging Your Secondary Classroom* (2022), *Lead Like a Teacher: How to Elevate Expertise in Your School* (2023), and *Writing Their Future Selves: Instructional Strategies to Affirm Student Identity* (2023). Her writing is widely represented across a broad range of education publications, and she is a frequent guest on education podcasts internationally. Plotinsky is a National Board Certified Teacher with additional certification in administration and supervision. She lives in Silver Spring, Maryland with her husband and three children, and can be found on her website at www.miriamplotinsky.com.